FUN AND FANTASTICAL

SLIPPERS
to KNIT

FUN AND FANTASTICAL
SLIPPERS *to* KNIT

mary scott huff

Creative Publishing
international

Creative Publishing international

Copyright © 2015 Creative Publishing international
Designs © 2015 Mary Scott Huff
Photography © 2015 Creative Publishing international

First published in the United States of America by
Creative Publishing international, a division of
Quarto Publishing Group USA Inc.
400 First Avenue North, Suite 400
Minneapolis, MN 55401

1-800-328-3895, www.creativepub.com

Visit www.Craftside.Typepad.com
for a behind-the-scenes peek at our crafty world!

ISBN: 978-1-58923-821-3

Digital edition published in 2015
eISBN: 978-1-62788-385-6

10 9 8 7 6 5 4 3 2 1

Library of Congress Cataloging-in-Publication Data available

Technical Editor: Karen Frisa
Copy Editor: Karen Levy
Proofreader: Kari Cornell
Cover and Book Design: Laura H. Couallier, Laura Herrmann Design
Illustrations: Michael Longfritz
Photographs: Nancy J. S. Langdon

Printed in China

CONTENTS

"It's easier to put on slippers than to carpet the world."

—Al Franken

ıNTRODUCTION

TWO LITTLE GIRLS ARE PLAYING IN THEIR MOTHER'S CLOSET. THE OLDER ONE HOLDS UP A SENSIBLE BLACK PUMP: "AND MAY I SUGGEST FOR MADAME SOMETHING IN A SNOWSHOE?" THE YOUNGER ONE GIGGLES BACK, "NO THANK YOU, MONSIEUR, YOU KNOW I POSITIVELY LOATHE A PURPLE SNOWSHOE."

And so it goes on, for hours and days. Mom's hiking boots are reimagined as dancing shoes. Her loafers become scuba flippers. Playing shoe store takes the imagination on vacation in a way that nothing else can.

To create the designs for this collection, I took a trip back to that imaginary shoe store in my mom's closet. You won't believe what I found in there.... Slippers for lounging, dancing, and doing battle. Slippers for silliness, self-reflection, and dashing through the snow. Animal, vegetable, and mineral: they're all here. Feel like a fox, or a fish? Professor or princess? Here are the slippers for you. Knitted or felted, buttoned or belted—there's a slipper here for every foot.

Slippers require less in the way of yarn, time, or commitment than other knitting projects. That makes them ideal gifts: fun to make, fun to receive. Especially if the recipient is you! Handmade slippers fit and feel better than anything you can buy. And then there's the customization: Need more durability? Add some soles. Need less coverage in the summer and more warmth in the winter? Make a seasonal slipper wardrobe. The only limits are the ones on your imagination.

You hold in your hand a key to the magical closet. Within you will find fantastical footwear for you and your loved ones. From boots to scuffs, and skimmers to loafers, there's a shape and size for you and everybody you knit for.

Dedication: For my sister, Susie, who taught me how to play shoe store.

SHEEPISH

**PEOPLE AND SHEEP HAVE ALWAYS NEEDED EACH OTHER.
NOW YOU CAN FINALLY HAVE YOUR VERY OWN FLOCK!**

Knit and felt a pair of simple scuffs, add ears and eyes, and then
work the fleeces in fun-to-knit loop stitch. Herd them around
when you feel like an alpha dog. Count them when it's time to
fall asleep. Pet their wool when you need comforting. See how
useful sheep are to have around? Not baaaaad.

Yarn

 Bulky

Shown: Ecological Wool by Cascade Yarns, 100% Peruvian Highland wool, 8.75 oz (250 g)/ 478 yd (437 m): Tarnish #8049 (MC), 1 skein; Vanilla #8014 (CC), 1 skein

Needles

Size 3 (3.25 mm)

Size 10 (6 mm) 24" (60 cm) circular

Size 11 (8 mm) set of dpn or size to obtain gauge

Notions

Stitch markers

Stitch holders

Tapestry needle

Hand sewing needle and thread

Four ½" (12 mm) buttons (shown: La Mode #20484)

1 yd (1 m) black worsted-weight yarn for embroidery

Gauge

13 sts and 17 rows = 4" (10 cm) in St st on largest needles, before felting

Take time to check gauge.

Sizes (refer to size chart, page 125)

Woman's S (Woman's M, Woman's L/Man's S, Man's M, Man's L, Man's XL)

Finished size: 8 (8½, 9, 9½, 10, 11)" (20.5 [21.5, 23, 24, 25.5, 28] cm) foot circumference, 8¾ (9½, 10, 10½, 11, 12)" (22 [24, 25.5, 26.5, 28, 30.5] cm) foot length

Note: Finished size is easily adjusted through blocking.

Construction: Slippers are worked from toe to heel, and then felted. Fleece is worked separately, and then appliquéd.

Stitch Guide: LS (Loop Stitch): K1, leaving st on left needle; bring yarn forward between needles, wrap around thumb once, then bring to back between needles; knit st on left needle again and drop st from left needle; pass first st over 2nd, securing loop.

Fleece Pattern (multiple of 2 sts):

Row 1 (RS): *K1, LS; rep from * to end of row.

Row 2 (WS): Purl.

Row 3: *LS, k1; rep from * to end of row.

Row 4: Purl.

Rep Rows 1–4 for patt.

SLIPPER

Toe

With MC, largest needle, and using Judy's magic CO or other toe-up method, CO 20 (20, 20, 24, 24, 24) sts—10 (10, 10, 12, 12, 12) sts on each of 2 dpn. Pm and join for working in rnds.

Next rnd: K10 (10, 10, 12, 12, 12), pm, k10 (10, 10, 12, 12, 12).

Inc rnd: *K1, M1R, knit to 1 st before marker, M1L, k1; rep from * once more—4 sts inc'd.

Rep inc rnd every other rnd 5 (6, 7, 7, 8, 9) more times—44 (48, 52, 56, 60, 64) sts. Work even in St st until piece measures 8 (8½, 9, 9½, 10, 11)" (20.5 [21.5, 23, 24, 25.5, 28] cm) from CO.

(continued)

Instep

Next rnd: K3 (4, 5, 5, 6, 7), place next 16 (16, 16, 18, 18, 18) sts on holder, turn—28 (32, 36, 38, 42, 46) sts.

Work back and forth in rows. Purl 1 WS row.

Dec row (RS): K1, ssk, knit to last 3 sts, k2tog, k1—2 sts dec'd.

Rep dec row every RS row 2 (3, 4, 4, 5, 6) more times—22 (24, 26, 28, 30, 32) sts.

Sole

Work even in St st until piece measures 14 (15, 16, 17, 18, 20)" (35.5 [38, 40.5, 43, 45.5, 51] cm) from CO, ending with a WS row. Rep dec row every RS row 3 (4, 5, 5, 6, 7) times—16 (16, 16, 18, 18, 18) sts. Place sts on holder.

Edging

With MC, middle-sized circular needle, RS facing, and beg at center of held sole sts, k8 (8, 8, 9, 9, 9), pick up and knit 29 (31, 33, 35, 37, 39) sts along left edge, k16 (16, 16, 18, 18, 18) held instep sts, pick up and knit 29 (31, 33, 35, 37, 39) sts along right edge, k8 (8, 8, 9, 9, 9) held sts—90 (94, 98, 106, 110, 114) sts. Break yarn and knot to beg of strand. With waste yarn and using a provisional method, CO 4 sts onto left needle, referring to Techniques chapter, page 120, for instructions. Join MC and work 4-st applied cord all the way around slipper, referring to Techniques chapter, page 123, for instructions. Break yarn and graft cord ends tog, referring to Techniques chapter, page 118, for instructions.

SHEEP

Ears (make 4)

With MC and largest needle, CO 3 sts. Purl 1 row.

Inc row (RS): K1, M1R, knit to last st, M1L, k1—2 sts inc'd.

Rep inc row every RS row 4 more times—13 sts. Work even in St st for 7 rows, ending with a WS row.

Dec row (RS): K1, ssk, knit to last 3 sts, k2tog, k1—2 sts dec'd.

Rep dec row every 4th row 2 more times—7 sts. Work 3 rows even in St st. BO.

Fleece (make 2)

With CC and smallest needle, CO 24 (26, 28, 30, 32, 36) sts. Work 10 (10, 10, 12, 12, 12) rows in fleece patt, ending with a WS row.

Next row (RS): Ssk, work 8 (9, 10, 10, 11, 13) sts in patt, BO 4 (4, 4, 6, 6, 6) sts, work in patt to last 2 sts, k2tog— 9 (10, 11, 11, 12, 14) sts each side.

Cont on left half of fleece only as foll:

Work 1 WS row.

Dec row (RS): Ssk, work in patt to last 2 sts, k2tog—2 sts dec'd.

Rep dec row every RS row 2 (3, 3, 3, 4, 5) more times—3 (2, 3, 3, 2, 2) sts. Work 1 WS row.

Next row (RS): Knit 3 (2, 3, 3, 2, 2) sts tog—1 st.

Break yarn and pull through last st. With WS facing, rejoin CC to right half of fleece. Work as for left half.

FINISHING

Weave in ends. Felt slippers (but not fleece), referring to Techniques chapter, page 114, for instructions. While still damp, shape slippers by hand to proper dimensions, cupping heels. Allow to dry completely. With toe of slipper pointing down, pin fleece to slipper with curved BO edge against instep cord edge. Sew in place invisibly by hand. Fold each ear in half vertically and sew narrow (BO) edges tog. Pin ears to slippers as shown and sew securely in place. Sew buttons in place for eyes. With black yarn, embroider nose and mouth as shown.

fLY AWAY HOME

LADY-BIRD, LADY-BIRD, FLY AWAY HOME

THE FIELD MOUSE IS GONE TO HER NEST

THE DAISIES HAVE SHUT UP THEIR SLEEPY RED EYES

AND THE BIRDS AND THE BEES ARE AT REST

LADY-BIRD, LADY-BIRD, FLY AWAY HOME

THE GLOW WORM IS LIGHTING HER LAMP

THE DEW'S FALLING FAST, AND YOUR FINE SPECKLED WINGS

WILL FLAG WITH THE CLOSE CLINGING DAMP

LADY-BIRD, LADY-BIRD, FLY AWAY HOME

THE FAIRY BELLS TINKLE AFAR

MAKE HASTE OR THEY'LL CATCH YOU AND HARNESS YOU FAST

WITH A COBWEB TO OBERON'S STAR

—Helen Ferris

Yarn

 Medium

Shown: Longwood by Cascade Yarns, 100% superwash extrafine merino wool, 3.5 oz (100 g) /191 yd (175 m): Red #04 (MC), 1 ball; Ebony #03 (CC), 1 ball

Needles

Size 5 (3.75 mm) set of dpn or size to obtain gauge

Size 4 (3.5 mm) set of dpn

Notions

Stitch markers

Tapestry needle

Hand sewing needle and thread

Two ¾" (19 mm) buttons for straps (shown: Slimline #397500084)

Four ⅜" (9 mm) buttons for eyes (shown: La Mode #29641)

Gauge

24 sts and 32 rows = 4" (10 cm) in St st on larger needle

Take time to check gauge.

Sizes (refer to size chart, page 125)

Child's S (Child's M, Child's L, Child's XL/ Woman's S)

Finished size: 6 (6¾, 6¾, 7¼)" (15 [17, 17, 18.5] cm) foot circumference, 6¼ (7¾, 8¼, 8¾)" (16 [19.5, 21, 22] cm) foot length

Note: Slippers are worked at a firmer gauge than that suggested by the yarn manufacturer.

Construction: Slippers are worked from toe to heel.

SLIPPER

Toe

With CC, larger dpn, and using Judy's magic CO or other toe-up method, CO 24 sts—12 sts on each of 2 dpn. Pm and join for working in rnds.

Next rnd: K12, pm, k12.

Inc rnd: *K2, M1R, knit to 2 sts before marker, M1L, k2; rep from * once more —4 sts inc'd.

Rep inc rnd every other rnd 2 (3, 3, 4) more times—36 (40, 40, 44) sts. Remove marker.
Knit 4 rnds. Change to MC. Knit 4 rnds.

Instep

Next rnd: K6 (6, 6, 7), BO 6 (8, 8, 8) sts, knit to end of rnd, then knit to BO sts—30 (32, 32, 36) sts.

Work back and forth in rows in St st.

Next row (WS): Purl.

Dec row (RS): K1, ssk, knit to last 3 sts, k2tog, k1—2 sts dec'd.

Rep dec row every RS row 2 more times—24 (26, 26, 30) sts. Work even until piece measures 3½ (5, 5½, 6)" (9 [12.5, 14, 15] cm) from CO, ending with a WS row.

Gusset

Inc row (RS): K2, M1R, knit to last 2 sts, M1L, k2—2 sts inc'd.

Rep inc row every RS row 2 more times—30 (32, 32, 36) sts.

Next row (WS): P5 (6, 6, 8), pm, purl to last 5 (6, 6, 8) sts, pm, p5 (6, 6, 8).

(continued)

Heel

Next short-row (RS): Knit to marker, wrap & turn.

Next short-row (WS): Purl to marker, wrap & turn.

Next short-row: Knit to 1 st before marker, wrap & turn.

Next short-row: Purl to 1 st before marker, wrap & turn.

Next short-row: Knit to 2 sts before marker, wrap & turn.

Next short-row: Purl to 2 sts before marker, wrap & turn.

Next short-row: Knit to 3 sts before marker, wrap & turn.

Next short-row: Purl to 3 sts before marker, wrap & turn.

Next short-row: Knit to 4 sts before marker, wrap & turn.

Next short-row: Purl to 4 sts before marker, wrap & turn.

Next short-row: Knit to 5 sts before marker, wrap & turn.

Next short-row: Purl to 5 sts before marker, wrap & turn.

Next short-row: Knit to 6 sts before marker, wrap & turn.

Next short-row: Purl to 6 sts before marker, wrap & turn.

Next short-row: Knit to marker, working wraps tog with wrapped sts, turn.

Next short-row: Purl to marker, working wraps tog with wrapped sts, turn.

Next short-row: Sl 1, knit to 1 st before marker, pm, ssk (removing marker), turn —1 st dec'd.

Next short-row: Sl 1, purl to 1 st before marker, pm, p2tog (removing marker), turn—1 st dec'd.

Next short-row: Sl 1, knit to marker, ssk, turn—1 st dec'd.

Next short-row: Sl 1, purl to marker, p2tog, turn—1 st dec'd.

Rep last 2 short-rows 3 (4, 4, 6) more times—20 sts.

Instep edging

With RS facing and smaller needle, k20 heel sts, then pick up and knit 56 (66, 70, 74) sts around instep edge —76 (86, 90, 94) sts. Pm and join for working in rnds. Work 4 rnds in k1, p1 rib. BO in patt.

STRAPS
Right slipper only

With MC, smaller needles, and RS facing, beg 2½ (3¼, 3½, 3¾)" (6.5 [8.5, 9, 9.5] cm) from center back of heel along left edge of instep edging, pick up and knit 7 sts through edge of ribbing.

Left slipper only

With MC, smaller needles, and RS facing, beg 3¼ (4, 4¼, 4½)" (8.5 [10, 11, 11.5] cm) from center back of heel along right edge of instep edging, pick up and knit 7 sts through edge of ribbing.

Both slippers

Work in k1, p1 rib until strap measures 1¾ (2, 2¼, 2½)" (4.5 [5, 5.5, 6.5] cm) from pick-up row, ending with a WS row.

Next row (RS): Work 2 sts in patt, BO 3 sts, work in patt to end.

Next row (WS): Work 2 sts in patt, CO 3 sts, work in patt to end.

Cont in patt until strap measures ½" (1.3 cm) from buttonhole. BO in patt.

LADYBUG

Antennae (make 4)

With smaller dpn and CC, CO 4 sts. Work knitted cord until piece measures 1¼" (3 cm), referring to Techniques chapter, page 122, for instructions.

Make bobble

Next row: K2, (knit into front, back, front, back, front, and back) of next st, turn—9 sts.

Next short-row (WS): P6, turn.

Next short-row (RS): K6, turn.

Rep last 2 short-rows once more. With RS facing, pass last 2nd, 3rd, 4th, 5th, and 6th sts over first, k1—4 sts. Break yarn and thread tail through rem sts. Fasten securely on inside of cord.

FINISHING

Weave in ends. With CC, embroider duplicate st spots as shown on chart, referring to Techniques chapter, page 119, for instructions, and referring to photo for placement. Sew larger button under strap at instep. Sew eye buttons and antennae in place as shown.

Stitch Pattern

SPOT

3

1

3 sts

KEY

☐ k with MC

☐ k with MC, duplicate st with CC

Little Piggy

This little piggy went to the yarn store

This little piggy stayed home (to knit)

This little piggy ate truffles

This little piggy had none
(she was blocking a shawl)

And this little piggy cried "Wee! Wee! Wee!
There's a sale at the yarn store!"
all the way home.

Best piglet fact:

Piglets prefer to sleep snuggled together, nose to nose.
Keep this in mind when you put your slippers in the closet.

Yarn

 Light

Shown: Socks that Rock Heavyweight by Blue Moon Fiber Arts, 100% superwash merino wool, 7 oz (198 g)/350 yd (320 m): Coral (MC), 1 skein; oddments of Rose Quartz (CA) and Chestnutty (CB)

Needles

Size 3 (3.25 mm) set of dpn or size to obtain gauge

Size 2 (2.75 mm) set of dpn

Notions

Stitch markers

Removable marker

Stitch holder

Tapestry needle

Hand sewing needle and thread

Four 7/16" (11 mm) buttons

Gauge

24 sts and 36 rows = 4" (10 cm) in St st on larger needles

Take time to check gauge.

Sizes (refer to size chart, page 125)

Child's S (M, L, XL)

Finished size: 6 (6¼, 7, 7¾)" (15 [16, 18, 19.5] cm) foot circumference, 5½ (7, 7¾, 8¼)" (14 [18, 19.5, 21] cm) foot length

Construction: Slippers are worked from heel to toe.

Stitch Guide: S2kp2: Sl 2 sts as if to k2tog, k1, p2sso—2 sts dec'd.

SLIPPER

Heel (make 2)

With larger needles and MC, CO 3 sts.

Next row (WS): P1, p1 and mark this st, p1.

Inc row (RS): Knit to marked st, M1R, k1 (marked st), M1L, knit to end of row—2 sts inc'd.

Rep inc row every other row 3 more times—11 sts. Work even in St st until piece measures 1½" (4 cm) from CO, ending with a WS row.

Dec row (RS): Knit to 1 st before marked st, s2kp2, knit to end of row —2 sts dec'd.

Work 3 rows even. Rep dec row—7 sts. Purl 1 row. Break yarn and place sts on holder.

Foot

With RS of heel facing, larger needles, and MC, pick up and knit 27 (29, 31, 33) sts evenly spaced around edge. Work even in St st until piece measures 2 (3½, 4, 4½)" (5 [9, 10, 11.5] cm) from pick-up row, ending with a RS row.

Toe

CO 9 (9, 11, 13) sts and join for working in rnds—36 (38, 42, 46) sts.

Next rnd: K5, pm for beg of rnd, k18 (19, 21, 23), pm, knit to end of rnd.

Work even in St st until piece measures 1½" (4 cm) from CO rnd.

Dec rnd: *K1, ssk, knit to 3 sts before marker, k2tog, k1; rep from * once more—4 sts dec'd.

Rep dec rnd every other rnd 4 (4, 5, 6) more times—16 (18, 18, 18) sts. Arrange sts evenly on 2 dpn. Graft toe, referring to Techniques chapter, page 118, for instructions.

Instep Edging

With smaller needles and MC, pick up and knit 15 (26, 29, 33) sts along left instep edge, 9 (9, 11, 13) sts along toe edge, 15 (26, 29, 33) sts along right instep edge, k7 held heel sts—46 (68, 76, 86) sts. Work 3 rnds k1, p1 rib. BO in patt.

PIGGY

Ears (make 4)

Outer ears

With larger needles and MC, CO 11 sts.

Next row (RS): K5, k1 and mark this st, k5.

Work 5 more rows in St st, ending with a WS row.

Dec row (RS): Knit to 1 st before marked st, s2kp2, knit to end of row —2 sts dec'd.

Rep dec row every 4th row once, then every RS row 3 times—1 st. Break yarn and pull through last st.

Inner ears

With larger needles and CA, CO 9 sts.

Next row (RS): K4, k1 and mark this st, k4.

Work 5 more rows in St st, ending with a WS row.

Dec row (RS): Knit to 1 st before marked st, s2kp2, knit to end of row —2 sts dec'd.

Rep dec row every 4th row once, then every RS row 2 times—1 st. Break yarn and pull through last st.

(continued)

Snout (make 2)

With larger needles and MC, leaving an 18" (45.5 cm) tail, CO 18 sts. Pm and join for working in rnds. Purl 1 rnd. Knit 4 rnds. Purl 1 rnd.

Next rnd: *K1, k2tog; rep from * to end of rnd—12 sts.

Knit 1 rnd.

Next rnd: *K2tog; rep from * to end of rnd—6 sts.

Break yarn and thread tail through rem sts. Fasten securely on WS.

Tail (make 2)

With larger needles and MC, CO 20 sts.

Next row: [K1f&b] 20 times—40 sts.

Purl 1 row. BO loosely.

Eyelids (make 4)

With larger needles and MC, CO 3 sts.

Next row (WS): P1, p1 and mark this st, p1.

Inc row (RS): Knit to marked st, M1R, k1 (marked st), M1L, knit to end of row—2 sts inc'd.

Rep inc row every RS row once more —7 sts. Work 5 rows even.

Dec row (RS): Knit to 1 st before marked st, s2kp2, knit to end of row —2 sts dec'd.

Rep dec row every RS row once more—3 sts.

Next row (WS): P3tog—1 st.

Break yarn and pull through last st.

Eyes (make 4)

With larger needles and CB, leaving a 12" (30.5 cm) tail, CO 6 sts. Work 6 rows in St st. Break yarn, leaving a 12" (30.5 cm) tail. With tail threaded on a tapestry needle, weave needle around lower 3 sides of square, then through 6 live sts, pulling slightly to gather. Wind CO tail into a ball and place in center of square to stuff. Pull gathering sts firmly to close bobble. Fasten securely, pulling tail to inside of bobble.

FINISHING

Wind CO tail into a ball and place inside snout to stuff. Weave in ends. With hand sewing needle and matching thread, sew snouts to slipper toes. Embroider nostrils on snouts with CB as shown. Tack eyelids to eyes at centers. Sew ends of eyelids to slipper tops. Sew buttons in centers of eyes. Fold each ear in half vertically to form pleat and stitch at base. Sew ears to slippers behind eyelids. Sew tails to heels as shown.

pEAS

THERE ARE SOCKS, AND THERE ARE SLIPPERS,
AND THEN THERE ARE SLIPPER SOCKS.

Not intended to be worn under shoes, slipper socks
offer the best of both worlds. Their high tops keep
drafts at bay, while their cozy feet stretch to fit like
socks do. Try these in the depths of winter, to help
you remember springtime in the garden.

Yarn

 Light

Shown: Socks that Rock Heavyweight by Blue Moon Fiber Arts, 100% superwash merino wool, 7 oz (198 g)/350 yd (320 m): Enchanted Forest (medium green; MC), 1 (1, 2, 2, 2) skein(s); Pistachio (light green; CC), 1 skein

Needles

Size 3 (3.25 mm) set of dpn or size to obtain gauge

Notions

Stitch markers

Removable markers

Stitch holder

Waste yarn for provisional CO

Tapestry needle

Crochet hook, size B/1 (2.25 mm)

Hand sewing needle and thread

Gauge

24 sts and 36 rnds = 4" (10 cm) in St st
Take time to check gauge.

Sizes (refer to size chart, page 125)

Woman's S (Woman's M, Woman's L, Woman's XL, Man's XL)

Finished size: 8 (8¾, 9¼, 9¼, 10)" (20.5 [22, 23.5, 23.5, 25.5] cm) foot circumference, 9 (10, 11, 11½, 12¼)" (23 [25.5, 28, 29, 31] cm) foot length

Note: To make this pattern in a child's size, use the instructions for Carrots, page 32 (omitting the root marks), then embellish as described here.

Construction: Slippers are worked from top to toe.

Stitch Guide: S2kp2: Sl 2 sts as if to k2tog, k1, p2sso—2 sts dec'd.

SLIPPER

Leg

With CC, CO 48 (52, 56, 56, 60) sts. Pm and join for working in rnds. Work 3 rnds in k1, p1 rib. Change to MC. Knit 1 rnd. Work 4 rnds in k1, p1 rib. Work in St st until piece measures 6½ (7, 7½, 9, 9½)" (16.5 [18, 19, 23, 24] cm) from CO.

Heel flap

Place last 24 (26, 28, 28, 30) sts of rnd on holder. Work heel flap back and forth in rows on first 24 (26, 28, 28, 30) sts of rnd as foll:

Row 1 (RS): *Sl 1, k1; rep from * to end of row.

Row 2 (WS): Sl 1, purl to end of row.

Rep Rows 1 and 2 for 11 (12, 13, 13, 14) more times, ending with a WS row—12 (13, 14, 14, 15) selvedge chain sts on each side of flap.

Heel turn

Row 1 (RS): Sl 1, k12 (14, 14, 14, 16), ssk, k1, turn.

Row 2 (WS): Sl 1, p3 (5, 3, 3, 5), p2tog, p1, turn.

Row 3 (RS): Sl 1, knit to 1 st before gap, ssk (1 st from each side of gap), k1, turn.

Row 4 (WS): Sl 1, purl to 1 st before gap, p2tog (1 st from each side of gap), p1, turn.

Rep Rows 3 and 4 for 3 (3, 4, 4, 4) more times, ending with a WS row—14 (16, 16, 16, 18) heel sts.

Gusset

Next row (RS): Sl 1, k13 (15, 15, 15, 17) heel sts, pick up and knit 12 (13, 14, 14, 15) sts along edge of heel flap, pm, k24 (26, 28, 28, 30) held instep sts, pm, pick up and knit 12 (13, 14, 14, 15) sts along edge of heel flap, k7 (8, 8, 8, 9) heel sts—62 (68, 72, 72, 78) sts.

Pm for beg of rnd; beg of rnd is at center of heel.

Rnd 1: Knit to 3 sts before marker, k2tog, k1, sl marker, knit to marker, k1, ssk, knit to end of rnd—2 sts dec'd.

Rnd 2: Knit.

Rep Rnds 1 and 2 for 6 (7, 7, 7, 8) more times—48 (52, 56, 56, 60) sts. Remove gusset markers.

Foot

Work even until piece measures 7½ (8, 8½, 9, 9½)" (19 [20.5, 21.5, 23, 24] cm) from center back of heel.

Toe

Set-up rnd: *K12 (13, 14, 14, 15), pm; rep from * to end of rnd.

Dec rnd: *K2tog, knit to marker; rep from * to end of rnd—4 sts dec'd.

Rep dec rnd every 4th rnd 10 (11, 12, 12, 13) more times—4 sts. Knit 3 rnds. Break yarn and thread tail through rem sts. Fasten securely on WS.

(continued)

Next rnd: *K1 and mark this st, k7; rep from * 2 more times.

Knit 3 rnds.

Dec rnd: *Knit to 1 st before marked st, s2kp2; rep from * 2 more times (last dec uses last st of rnd and first 2 sts of next rnd)—6 sts dec'd.

Rep dec rnd every 4th rnd 2 more times—6 sts. Knit 3 rnds.

Next rnd: [K2tog] 3 times—3 sts.

Work 3-st cord for 6 rows, referring to Techniques chapter, page 122, for instructions. Break yarn and thread tail through rem sts. Fasten securely on WS.

Large leaves (make 2)

With CC and leaving a 12" (30.5 cm) tail, CO 3 sts.

Next row (WS): P1, p1 and mark this st, p1.

Inc row (RS): Knit to 1 st before marked st, M1R, k1 (marked st), M1L, knit to end of row—2 sts inc'd.

Rep inc row every RS row 5 more times—15 sts. Work 3 rows in St st.

Dec row (RS): Knit to 1 st before marked st, s2kp2, knit to end of row —2 sts dec'd.

Rep dec row every 4th row 3 more times—7 sts. Rep dec row every RS row 3 times—1 st. Break yarn and pull through last st. Crochet CO tail into short chain and twist into a spiral with fingers.

PEA POD EMBELLISHMENTS
Pea pod tops (make 2)
Leaves (make 3)

With waste yarn, CC, and using a provisional method, CO 9 sts, referring to Techniques chapter, page 120, for instructions.

Next row (RS): K4, k1 and mark this st, k4.

Work 3 more rows in St st, ending with a WS row.

Dec row (RS): Knit to 1 st before marked st, s2kp2, knit to end of row—2 sts dec'd.

Rep dec row every 4th row 3 more times—1 st. Break yarn and pull through last st.

Pod tip

Remove waste yarn from provisional CO and place 8 live sts onto each of 3 dpn—24 sts. Pm and join for working in rnds.

Small leaves (make 4)

With CC and leaving a 12" (30.5 cm) tail, CO 3 sts.

Next row (WS): P1, p1 and mark this st, p1.

Inc row (RS): Knit to 1 st before marked st, M1R, k1 (marked st), M1L, knit to end of row—2 sts inc'd.

Rep inc row every RS row 3 more times—11 sts. Work 3 rows in St st.

Dec row (RS): Knit to 1 st before marked st, s2kp2, knit to end of row —2 sts dec'd.

Rep dec row every 4th row 2 more times—5 sts. Rep dec row every RS row 2 times—1 st. Break yarn and pull through last st. Crochet CO tail into short chain and twist into a spiral with fingers.

Pod edges (make 2)

With CC, CO 4 sts. Work 4-st knitted cord for 12" (30.5 cm). Break yarn and thread tail through rem sts. Fasten securely on WS.

Peas (make 10)

With CC and leaving a 2 yd (2 m) tail, CO 8 sts. Work 8 rows in St st. Break yarn, leaving a 12" (30.5 cm) tail. With tail threaded on a tapestry needle, weave needle around lower 3 sides of square, then through 8 live sts, pulling slightly to gather. Wind CO tail into a ball and place in center of square to stuff. Pull gathering sts firmly to close bobble. Fasten securely, pulling tail to inside of bobble.

Tendrils (make 6)

With CC and crochet hook, make chains of random lengths as shown. Curl into corkscrews with fingers as shown.

FINISHING

Weave in ends. Pin pea pod tops to toes and tack in place with hand sewing needle and thread. Fold pod edges in half and sew ends tog. Pin pod edges to top of instep and tack in place, taking care not to compromise stretch of knitted fabric. Pin and sew peas in place inside pod edges, as shown. Tack 1 large and 2 small leaves onto each slipper, as shown. Tack tendrils in place.

CARROTS ......

THE REASON THAT PEAS AND CARROTS GO
TOGETHER IS THAT THEY ARE FRIENDS IN THE
GARDEN. THEIR ROOT ZONES OVERLAP NICELY,
THEIR SUNLIGHT AND WATER NEEDS ARE SIMILAR,
AND THEIR GROWING SEASONS ARE THE SAME.

No wonder they end up on the same plate. Peas
and Carrots slipper socks are perfect for people
who get along famously.

Yarn

 Light

Shown: Socks that Rock Heavyweight by Blue Moon Fiber Arts, 100% superwash merino wool, 7 oz (198 g)/350 yd (320 m): Cozy Fierce and Dirty Orange (MC), 1 skein; Enchanted Forest (CC), 1 skein

Needles

Size 3 (3.25 mm) set of dpn or size to obtain gauge

Notions

Stitch markers

Stitch holder

Tapestry needle

Hand sewing needle and thread

Gauge

24 sts and 36 rnds = 4" (10 cm) in St st

Take time to check gauge.

Sizes (refer to size chart, page 125)

Child's S (M, L, XL)

Finished size: 6 (6¾, 7¼, 8)" (15 [17, 18.5, 20.5] cm) foot circumference, 6 (7, 8, 9)" (15 [18, 20.5, 23] cm) foot length

Note: To make this pattern in an adult's size, use the instructions for Peas, page 26 (adding root marks), then embellish as described here.

Construction: Slippers are worked from top to toe.

SLIPPER

Leg

With CC, CO 36 (40, 44, 48) sts. Pm and join for working in rnds. Work 3 rnds in k1, p1 rib. Change to MC. Knit 1 rnd. Work 4 rnds in k1, p1 rib. Work in St st until piece measures 4½ (5, 5½, 6)" (11.5 [12.5, 14, 15] cm) from CO, purling 1–7 sts at random intervals, as shown, for root marks.

Heel flap

Place last 18 (20, 22, 24) sts of rnd on holder. Work heel flap back and forth in rows on first 18 (20, 22, 24) sts of rnd as foll:

Row 1 (RS): *Sl 1, k1; rep from * to end of row.

Row 2 (WS): Sl 1, purl to end of row.

Rep Rows 1 and 2 for 8 (9, 10, 11) more times, ending with a WS row—9 (10, 11, 12) selvedge chain sts on each side of flap.

Heel turn

Row 1 (RS): Sl 1, k8 (10, 12, 14), ssk, k1, turn.

Row 2 (WS): Sl 1, p1 (3, 5, 7), p2tog, p1, turn.

Row 3 (RS): Sl 1, knit to 1 st before gap, ssk (1 st from each side of gap), k1, turn.

Row 4 (WS): Sl 1, purl to 1 st before gap, p2tog (1 st from each side of gap), p1, turn.

Rep Rows 3 and 4 twice more, ending with a WS row—10 (12, 14, 16) heel sts.

(continued)

Gusset

Next row (RS): Sl 1, k9 (11, 13, 15) heel sts, pick up and knit 9 (10, 11, 12) sts along edge of heel flap, pm, k18 (20, 22, 24) held instep sts, pm, pick up and knit 9 (10, 11, 12) sts along edge of heel flap, k5 (6, 7, 8) heel sts—46 (52, 58, 64) sts.

Pm for beg of rnd; beg of rnd is at center of heel.

Rnd 1: Knit to 3 sts before marker, k2tog, k1, sl marker, knit to marker, k1, ssk, knit to end of rnd—2 sts dec'd.

Rnd 2: Knit, purling at random intervals on instep (top of foot) only.

Rep Rnds 1 and 2 for 4 (5, 6, 7) more times—36 (40, 44, 48) sts. Remove gusset markers.

Foot

Work even until piece measures 4½ (5, 5½, 6)" (11.5 [12.5, 14, 15] cm) from center back of heel, cont to purl randomly on instep.

Toe

Set-up rnd: *K9 (10, 11, 12), pm; rep from * to end of rnd.

Dec rnd: *K2tog, knit to marker; rep from * to end of rnd—4 sts dec'd.

Rep dec rnd every 4th rnd 7 (8, 9, 10) more times—4 sts. Knit 3 rnds. Break yarn and thread tail through rem sts. Fasten securely on WS.

CARROT EMBELLISHMENTS

Small leaves (make 2)

With CC, CO 20 sts. BO 3 sts—17 sts. [Sl last st to left needle, CO 3 sts, BO 6 sts] 2 times—11 sts. [Sl last st to left needle, CO 5 sts, BO 8 sts] 2 times—5 sts. BO.

Medium leaves (make 4)

With CC, CO 25 sts. BO 3 sts—22 sts. [Sl last st to left needle, CO 3 sts, BO 6 sts] 2 times—16 sts. [Sl last st to left needle, CO 5 sts, BO 8 sts] 2 times—10 sts. [Sl last st to left needle, CO 7 sts, BO 10 sts] 2 times—4 sts. BO.

Large leaves (make 2)

With CC, CO 30 sts. BO 3 sts—27 sts. [Sl last st to left needle, CO 3 sts, BO 6 sts] 2 times—21 sts. [Sl last st to left needle, CO 5 sts, BO 8 sts] 2 times—15 sts. [Sl last st to left needle, CO 7 sts, BO 10 sts] 2 times—9 sts. [Sl last st to left needle, CO 9 sts, BO 12 sts] 2 times—3 sts. BO.

FINISHING

Weave in ends. Pin 1 small, 2 medium, and 1 large leaf to top of leg on left side. Sew in place with hand sewing needle and matching thread. Rep for 2nd slipper, reversing location.

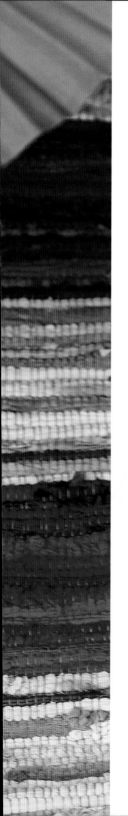

KIMONO

THE JAPANESE WORD *KIMONO* TRANSLATES TO "THING TO WEAR." SO IT'S PERFECTLY CORRECT TO SAY YOU'VE KNITTED KIMONO FOR YOUR FEET.

Simple to knit and elegant to wear, Kimono slippers work up quickly and require almost no finishing. You can observe Japanese tradition by matching your Kimono to the seasons of the year: dark for winter, pale for spring, bright for summer, and russet for autumn.

Yarn

 Medium

Shown: Tosh Vintage by Madelinetosh, 100% superwash merino wool, 3.5 oz (100 g)/ 200 yd (183 m): Flash Dance (MC), 1 (1, 2, 2, 2) skein(s); Maple Leaf (CC), 1 skein

Needles

Size 5 (3.75 mm) set of dpn or size to obtain gauge

Size 4 (3.5 mm) 24" (60 cm) circular

Size 4 (3.5 mm) set of dpn

Notions

Stitch markers

Stitch holder

Tapestry needle

Hand sewing needle and thread

Four ⅞" (22 mm) buttons (shown: JHB #72046)

Gauge

24 sts and 32 rows = 4" (10 cm) in St st on larger needles

Take time to check gauge.

Sizes (refer to size chart, page 125)

Woman's S (Woman's M, Woman's L/ Man's S, Woman's XL/Man's M, Man's L)

Finished size: 6¾ (7¼, 8, 8¾, 9¼)" (17 [18.5, 20.5, 22, 23.5] cm) foot circumference, 8¼ (9, 9¾, 10½, 11¼)" (21 [23, 25, 26.5, 28.5] cm) foot length

Note: Slippers are worked at a firmer gauge than that suggested by the yarn manufacturer.

Construction: Slippers are worked from heel to toe.

SLIPPER

Heel

With larger dpn, MC, and using Judy's magic CO or other toe-up method, CO 32 sts—16 sts on each of 2 dpn.

Next row (RS): K16, pm, k16, turn.

Working back and forth in rows, cont as foll:

Purl 1 row.

Inc row (RS): Knit to 1 st before marker, M1R, k2, M1L, knit to end of row—2 sts inc'd.

Rep inc row every RS row 3 (5, 7, 9, 11) more times—40 (44, 48, 52, 56) sts. Remove marker.

Foot

Work even in St st until piece measures 5 (5½, 6, 6½, 7)" (12.5 [14, 15, 16.5, 18] cm) from CO, ending with a WS row.

Inc row (RS): K1, M1R, knit to last st, M1L, k1—2 sts inc'd.

Rep inc row every RS row 7 more times—56 (60, 64, 68, 72) sts. Place sts on holder.

Edging

With RS facing, circular needle, and CC, pick up and knit 98 (102, 106, 110, 114) sts along selvedge edge of foot. Break yarn.

Left slipper only

With smaller dpn and CC, CO 4 sts. Work 4-st knitted cord for 14 rows, referring to Techniques chapter, page 122, for instructions. Work 4-st applied knitted cord, joining to picked-up sts, referring to Techniques chapter, page 123, for instructions.

Right slipper only

With smaller dpn and CC, CO 4 sts. Work 4-st applied knitted cord, joining to picked-up sts, referring to Techniques chapter, page 123, for instructions. After all picked-up sts have been worked, work knitted cord for 14 more rows, referring to Techniques chapter, page 122, for instructions.

Both slippers

Break yarn and thread tail through sts. Pull tail to inside of cord.

Toe

Arrange foot sts on 3 larger dpn.

Left slipper only

Overlap 16 sts at end of row over 16 sts at beg of row. Join MC after overlapped sts.

Next rnd: K24 (28, 32, 36, 40), [k2tog (1 st from front dpn with 1 st from back dpn)] 16 times—40 (44, 48, 52, 56) sts.

Next rnd: K2 (3, 4, 5, 6), pm for new beg of rnd, k20 (22, 24, 26, 28), pm, knit to end of rnd.

Right slipper only

Overlap 16 sts at beg of row over 16 sts at end of row. Join MC before overlapped sts.

Next rnd: [K2tog (1 st from front dpn with 1 st from back dpn)] 16 times, knit to end of rnd—40 (44, 48, 52, 56) sts.

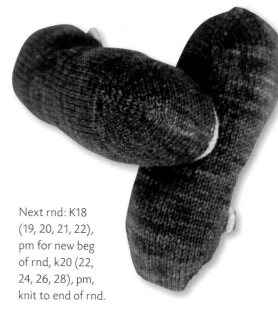

Next rnd: K18 (19, 20, 21, 22), pm for new beg of rnd, k20 (22, 24, 26, 28), pm, knit to end of rnd.

Both slippers

Knit 3 rnds.

Dec rnd: *K1, ssk, knit to 3 sts before marker, k2tog, k1; rep from * once more—4 sts dec'd.

Rep dec rnd every other rnd 3 (4, 5, 6, 7) more times—24 sts. Arrange sts evenly on 2 dpn. Graft toe, referring to Techniques chapter, page 118, for instructions.

FINISHING

Weave in ends. With smaller needles and CC, CO 4 sts. Work knitted cord for 14 rows. Break yarn and thread tail through sts. Pull tail to inside of cord. Make a second cord to match. Bend end of instep edging cord underneath itself to form button loop and sew in place with hand sewing needle and thread. Sew ends of small cord tog and sew to instep edging cord as shown. Sew buttons under button loops. Steam slippers lightly to block.

tURKISH DELIGHT

A LITTLE RESEARCH ON THE TOPIC OF TURKISH SLIPPERS WILL YIELD INFORMATION ON TWO TYPES OF SLIPPERS: SLIP-ON SCUFFS WITH UPTURNED TOES, AND HAND-KNITTED BEAUTIES WORKED IN STRANDED COLORWORK PATTERNS.

This pair combines both styles. Scuffs are fun to knit because there's only the toe and flat sole to make. A little stuffing keeps those pointy toes headed skyward, and smooth knitted cord finishes the edges. Soft insoles pad the bottoms, while deer-hide soles protect them. A sweet treat for your favorite feet!

Yarn

 Light

Shown: Tosh Merino DK by Madelinetosh, 100% superwash merino wool, 3.5 oz (100 g) /225 yd (206 m): Amber Trinket (MC), 1 skein; Duchess (CA), 1 skein; Forestry (CB), 1 skein

Needles

Size 3 (3.25 mm) set of dpn or size to obtain gauge

Size 3 (3.25 mm) 16" (40 cm) circular

Notions

Stitch marker

Waste yarn for provisional CO

Stitch holders

Tapestry needle

Hand sewing needle and thread

Wool roving or other stuffing

12" × 12" (30.5 × 30.5 cm) sheet chipboard

Foam shoe insoles

Deer hide

Gauge

28 sts and 30 rnds = 4" (10 cm) in 2-color stranded St st

Take time to check gauge.

Sizes (refer to size chart, page 125)

Woman's S (Woman's M, Woman's L/Man's S, Woman's XL/Man's M)

Finished size: 7¾ (8¼, 8¾, 9½)" (19.5 [21, 22, 24] cm) foot circumference, 8¾ (9¾, 10½, 11¼)" (22 [25, 26.5, 28.5] cm) foot length

SLIPPER

Toe

Using a provisional method, CO 54 (58, 62, 66) sts, referring to Techniques chapter, page 120, for instructions. Pm and join for working in rnds. With MC, knit 2 rnds. Work Rows 1–50 of Turkish Delight chart (pages 48–51) for your size—5 (6, 6, 6) sts. Break yarn and thread tail through rem sts. Fasten securely on WS.

Inner toe panel

Turn slipper WS out. With MC and beg at right edge of slipper, pick up and knit 26 sts through purl bumps of chart Row 37 (last row of colorwork). Knit 1 rnd.

Next rnd: K5, [k2tog] 8 times, k5—18 sts.

Knit 1 rnd. Stuff slipper toe with wool roving or other stuffing. Arrange 9 sts evenly on each of 2 dpn. Work 3-needle BO to close, referring to Techniques chapter, page 122, for instructions. Pull ends to inside of stuffing. Turn slipper RS out. With MC threaded on a tapestry needle, work a row of running sts from top center colorwork motif to point of toe and back. Pull yarn ends firmly to gather, then fasten securely on WS.

Sole

Note: Sole is worked in St st with MC. When worn, purl side of sole (WS) will face bottom of foot, with knit side (RS) facing floor.

Remove waste yarn from provisional CO, placing center 19 sts on holder for instep point, and rem 35 (39, 43, 47) sts arranged evenly on 2 dpn. With MC, cont as foll:

Dec row (RS): K1, ssk, knit to last 3 sts, k2tog, k1—2 sts dec'd.

Rep dec row every RS row 7 (8, 9, 10) more times—19 (21, 23, 25) sts. Work even in St st until piece measures 3½ (4, 4½, 5)" (9 [10, 11.5, 12.5] cm) from first dec row, ending with a WS row. Rep dec row on next row, then every other row 3 (4, 5, 6) more times—11 sts. Place sts on holder.

Instep point

With RS facing and MC, work 19 held sts of instep as foll:

Dec row (RS): K1, ssk, knit to last 3 sts, k2tog, k1—2 sts dec'd.

Dec row (WS): P1, p2tog, purl to last 3 sts, ssp, p1—2 sts dec'd.

Rep last 2 rows 2 more times, then work RS dec row once more—5 sts.

Next row (WS): P1, s2pp2, p1—3 sts.

Next row: S2kp2—1 st.

Break yarn and pull through last st.

(continued)

Edging

With circular needle, CB, and WS of sole facing, k11 held sole sts, pick up and knit 43 (46, 49, 52) sts along side of sole, ending at instep point, then pick up and knit 43 (46, 49, 52) sts along second side of sole—97 (103, 109, 115) sts. With waste yarn, dpn, and using a provisional method, CO 4 sts. With CB, work 4-st applied knitted cord (referring to Techniques chapter, page 123, for instructions) to instep point, then work 4 rows unattached knitted cord, then work attached knitted cord to end. Remove waste yarn from beg of cord and place 4 live sts onto dpn. Graft ends of cord tog, referring to Techniques chapter, page 118, for instructions.

BOBBLES (Make 6)

With CB and leaving a 12" (30.5 cm) tail, CO 6 sts. Work 6 rows in St st. Break yarn, leaving a 12" (30.5 cm) tail. With tail threaded on a tapestry needle, weave needle around lower 3 sides of square, then through 6 live sts, pulling slightly to gather. Wind CO tail into a ball and place in center of square to stuff. Pull gathering sts firmly to close bobble. Fasten securely, pulling tail to inside of bobble. With hand sewing needle and thread, sew 3 bobbles tog, forming a cluster, then sew to slipper toe.

SOLES

Trace around foot to make sole pattern. Fold tracing in half vertically and trim evenly with scissors. Trace pattern onto chipboard and foam insoles; cut out soles. Gently bend toe end of chipboard to curl. Trace pattern onto WS of deer hide. Trace again ¼" (6 mm) outside first line. Cut out leather soles on second line. Layer pieces and sew to RS of slipper, referring to Techniques chapter, page 117, for instructions.

(continued)

Turkish Delight Charts

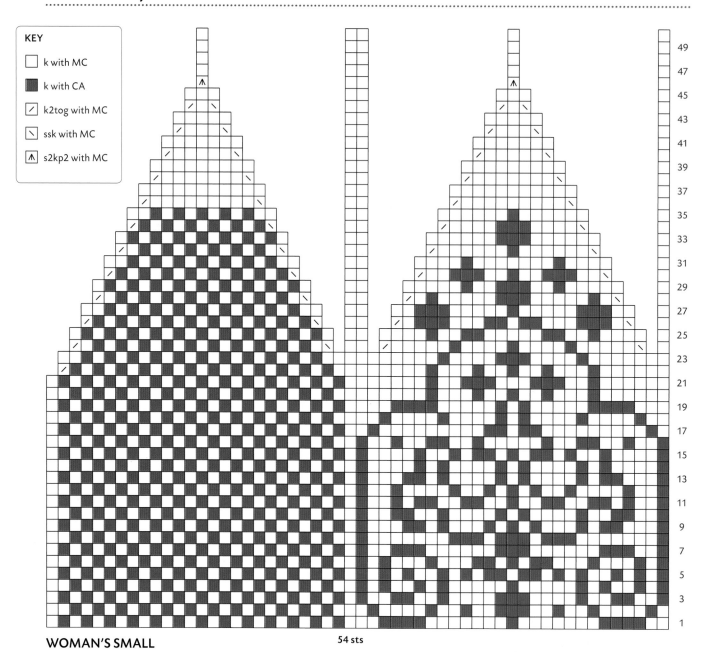

KEY

- ☐ k with MC
- ■ k with CA
- ╱ k2tog with MC
- ╲ ssk with MC
- ⋀ s2kp2 with MC

49
47
45
43
41
39
37
35
33
31
29
27
25
23
21
19
17
15
13
11
9
7
5
3
1

WOMAN'S SMALL

54 sts

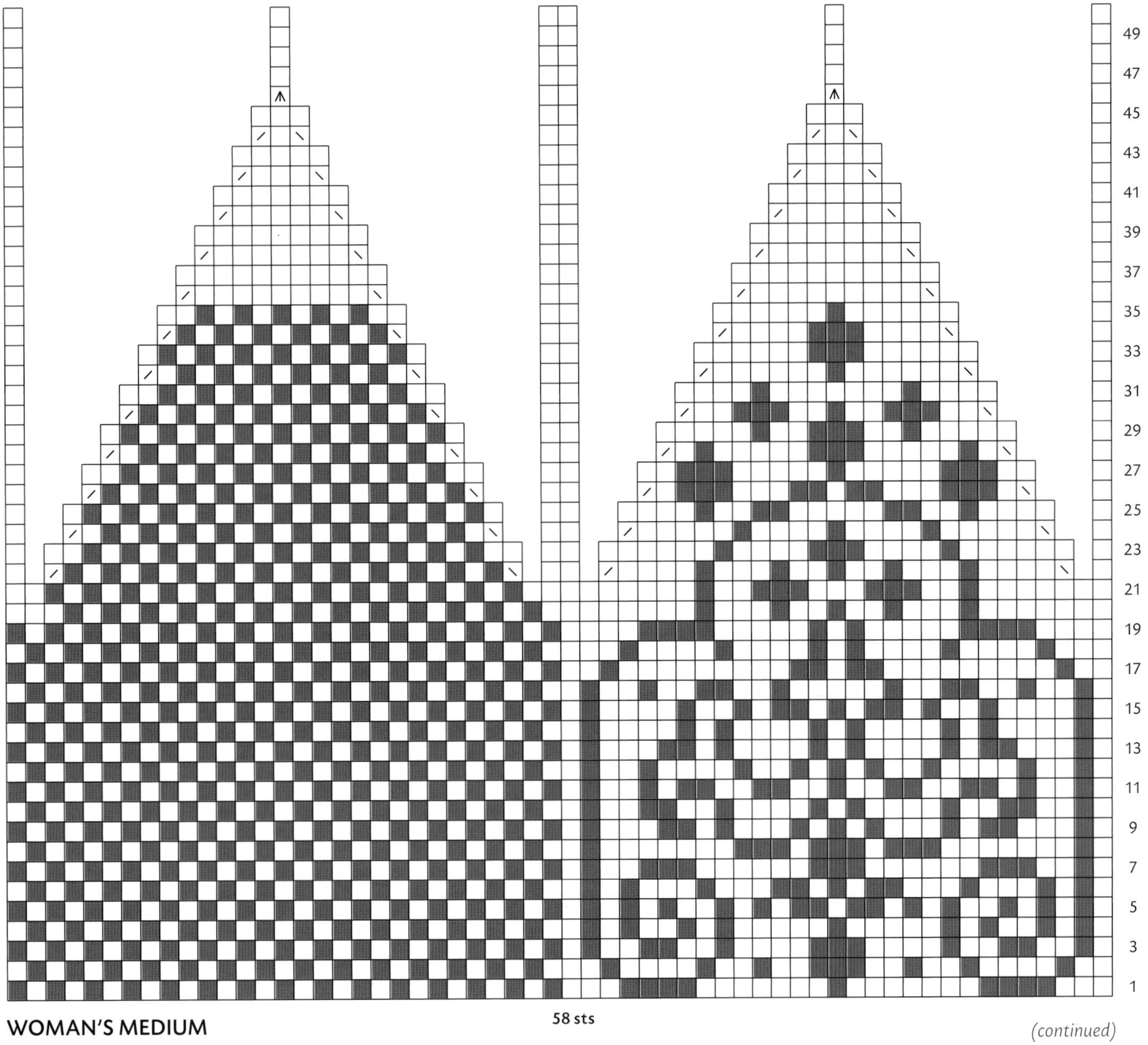

WOMAN'S MEDIUM

58 sts

(continued)

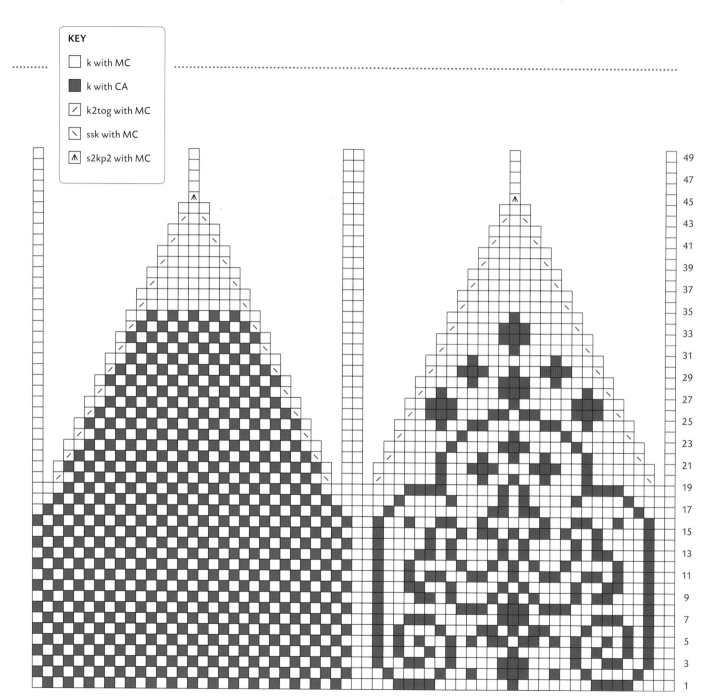

WOMAN'S LARGE/MAN'S SMALL

62 sts

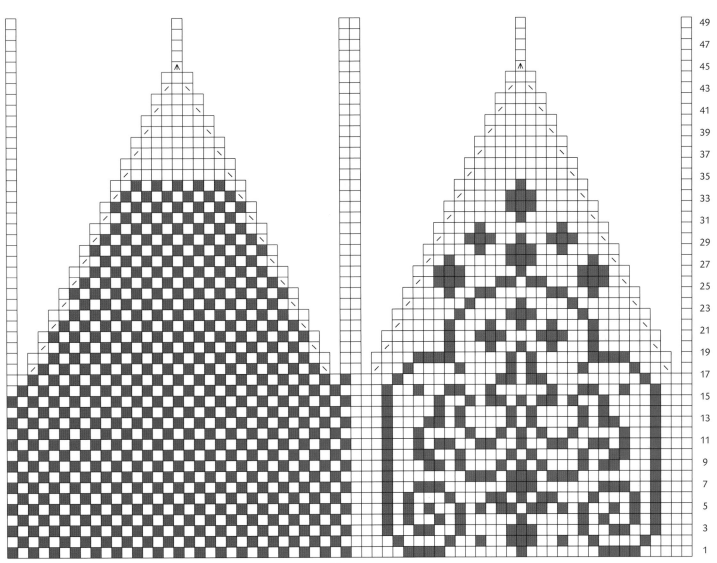

WOMAN'S X-LARGE/MAN'S MEDIUM

66 sts

49
47
45
43
41
39
37
35
33
31
29
27
25
23
21
19
17
15
13
11
9
7
5
3
1

foxy

From ancient Mesopotamian legends to modern Dr. Seuss, people have been telling stories about foxes. Their cleverness and cunning fascinate us endlessly, while their accidents and foibles remind us of our own frailties. All right then, all you tods and vixens: wear this pair when you feel foxy.

Yarn

 Bulky

Shown: Eco+ by Cascade Yarns, 100% Peruvian Highland wool, 8.75 oz (250 g)/478 yd (437 m): Pumpkin Spice #2453 (MC), 1 skein

Ecological Wool by Cascade Yarns, 100% Peruvian Highland wool, 8.75 oz (250 g)/478 yd (437 m): Vanilla #8014 (CC), 1 skein

Needles

Size 11 (8 mm) 16" (40 cm) circular or size to obtain gauge

Size 11 (8 mm) set of dpn

Notions

Stitch markers

Removable marker

Tapestry needle

Waste yarn for provisional CO

Hand sewing needle and thread

Two ¾" (20 mm) buttons (shown: JHB #60235)

Two ⁹⁄₁₆" (13 mm) buttons (shown: La Mode #2065)

Four ⅜" (9 mm) buttons (shown: La Petite #735)

Gauge

13 sts and 17 rows = 4" (10 cm) in St st with MC, before felting

Take time to check gauge.

Sizes (refer to size chart, page 125)

Woman's S (Woman's M, Woman's L/Man's S, Man's M, Man's L)

Finished size: 7¾ (8½, 9, 9½, 10)" (19.5 [21.5, 23, 24, 25.5] cm) foot circumference, 8¾ (9½, 10, 10½, 11)" (22 [24, 25.5, 26.5, 28] cm) foot length

Note: Finished size is easily adjusted through blocking.

Construction: Slippers are worked from heel to toe, then felted.

Stitch Guide: S2kp2: Sl 2 sts as if to k2tog, k1, p2sso—2 sts dec'd.

SLIPPER

Heel (make 2)

With MC, CO 3 sts.

Next row (WS): P1, p1 and mark this st, p1.

Inc row (RS): Knit to marked st, M1R, k1 (marked st), M1L, knit to end of row—2 sts inc'd.

Rep inc row every RS row 3 more times—11 sts.

Work even in St st until piece measures 7 (7½, 8, 8½, 9)" (18 [19, 20.5, 21.5, 23] cm) from CO, ending with a WS row.

Dec row (RS): Knit to 1 st before marked st, s2kp2, knit to end of row—2 sts dec'd.

Rep dec row every RS row 4 more times —1 st. Break yarn and pull through last st.

Foot

With circular needle, MC, RS facing, and beg 3" (7.5 cm) down from top point of heel, pick up and knit 14 (16, 18, 20, 22) sts along left edge, 1 st at center bottom, and 14 (16, 18, 20, 22) sts along right edge, ending 3" (7.5 cm) from top point—29 (33, 37, 41, 45) sts.

Work back and forth in St st until piece measures 6½ (7, 7, 7½, 8)" (16.5 [18, 18, 19, 20.5] cm) from center back of heel, ending with a WS row.

Right slipper only

Inc row (RS): K1, M1R, knit to end of row—1 st inc'd.

Rep inc row every RS row 4 more times—34 (38, 42, 46, 50) sts. Work 1 WS row.

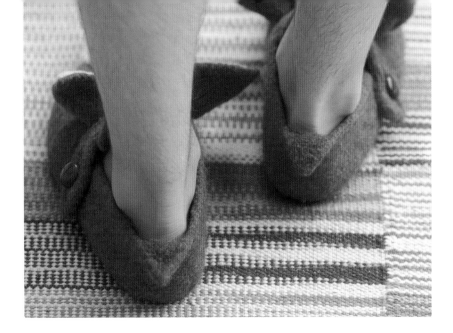

Right strap: Work back and forth over first 10 sts as foll:

Next row (RS): K1, M1R, k6, k2tog, k1, turn.

Next row (WS): Purl.

Rep last 2 rows until strap measures 7 (7½, 8, 8½, 9)" (18 [19, 20.5, 21.5, 23] cm), ending with a WS row.

Dec row (RS): K1, ssk, knit to last 3 sts, k2tog, k1—2 strap sts dec'd.

Rep dec row every RS row 2 more times—4 strap sts. Work 1 WS row.

Next row (RS): Ssk, k2tog—2 strap sts.

Next row (WS): P2tog—1 strap st.

Break yarn and pull through last st—24 (28, 32, 36, 40) foot sts.

Left slipper only

Inc row (RS): Knit to last st, M1L, k1— 1 st inc'd.

Rep inc row every RS row 4 more times—34 (38, 42, 46, 50) sts. Work 1 WS row.

Left strap: Next row (RS): Knit to last 10 sts, k1, ssk, k6, M1L, k1.

Work back and forth over last 10 sts as foll:

Next row (WS): P10, turn.

Next row (RS): K1, ssk, k6, M1L, k1.

Rep last 2 rows until strap measures 7 (7, 8, 8, 9)" (18 [19, 20.5, 21.5, 23] cm), ending with a WS row.

Dec row (RS): K1, ssk, knit to last 3 sts, k2tog, k1—2 strap sts dec'd.

Rep dec row every RS row 2 more times—4 strap sts. Work 1 WS row.

Next row (RS): Ssk, k2tog—2 strap sts.

Next row (WS): P2tog—1 strap st.

Break yarn and pull through last st—24 (28, 32, 36, 40) foot sts.

(continued)

Tongue (make 2)

With MC and dpn, CO 10 sts. Purl 1 row.

Inc row (RS): K1, M1R, knit to last st, M1L, k1—2 sts inc'd.

Rep inc row every RS row 4 more times—20 sts. Work even in St st until piece measures 4 (4½, 5, 5½, 6)" (10 [11.5, 12.5, 14, 15] cm) from CO, ending with a RS row. With RS facing, k24 (28, 32, 36, 40) foot sts and join for working in rnds—44 (48, 52, 56, 60) sts.

Next rnd: K21 (22, 23, 24, 25), pm, k22 (24, 26, 28, 30), pm for new beg of rnd.

Toe

Work in St st until piece measures 13 (14, 14½, 15, 16)" (33 [35.5, 37, 38, 40.5] cm) from center back of heel.

Dec rnd: *K1, ssk, knit to 3 sts before marker, k2tog, k1; rep from * once more—4 sts dec'd.

Rep dec rnd every other rnd 4 (5, 6, 7, 8) more times—24 sts. Graft toe, referring to Techniques chapter, page 118, for instructions.

EARS (make 4)

With MC, CO 15 sts. Work 3 rows in St st, beg with a purl row.

Dec row (RS): K1, ssk, knit to last 3 sts, k2tog, k1—2 sts dec'd.

Rep dec row every RS row 4 more times—5 sts. Work 1 WS row.

Next row (RS): Ssk, k1, k2tog—3 sts.

Work 1 WS row.

Next row (RS): S2kp2—1 st.

Break yarn and pull through last st.

Ear linings (make 4)

With CC, CO 13 sts. Work as for ears, rep first dec row 3 more times, rather than 4.

FOX

Muzzle (make 2)

With waste yarn and using a provisional method, CO 11 sts, referring to Techniques chapter, page 120, for instructions. With CC, work 3 rows in St st, beg with a knit row.

Next row (WS): P5, p1 and mark this st, p5.

Dec row (RS): Knit to 1 st before marked st, s2kp2, knit to end of row—2 sts dec'd.

Rep dec row every RS row 4 more times—1 st. Break yarn and pull through last st. Remove waste yarn from provisional CO and place 10 live sts onto needle. Rejoin CC.

Inc row (RS): K1, M1R, knit to last st, M1L, k1—2 sts inc'd.

Rep inc row every RS row once more—14 sts. With RS facing, CO 14 sts onto right needle, pm, and join for working in rnds—28 sts. Knit 2 rnds.

Next rnd: *K7, pm; rep from * to end of rnd.

Dec rnd: *Knit to 2 sts before marker, k2tog; rep from * to end of rnd—4 sts dec'd.

Rep dec rnd every 3rd rnd 4 more times—8 sts. Knit 2 rnds. Break yarn and thread tail through rem sts. Fasten securely on WS.

FINISHING

Weave in ends. Felt all pieces, referring to Techniques chapter, page 114, for instructions. While still damp, stretch, mold, and shape pieces to desired measurements. Allow to dry completely. Layer ear lining over ear with WS tog and lower edges even. Sew tog invisibly by hand with matching thread.

Fold ear in half vertically and tack lower edge tog halfway from fold. Stuff end of muzzle lightly with leftover yarn and pin in place at end of slipper toe. Sew in place. Open ears and sew in place as shown. Sew eye and nose buttons in place. At end of strap, cut a slash for buttonhole to fit button. Reinforce buttonhole with buttonhole stitching, referring to Techniques chapter, page 120, for instructions. Try on slippers and mark button placement. Sew buttons under buttonholes.

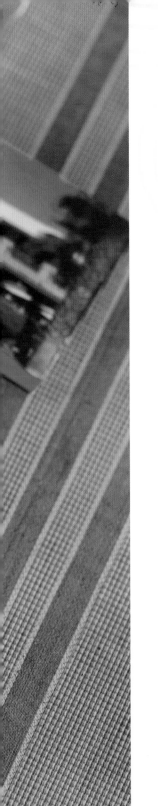

Smoking Slippers

AH, THE GILDED AGE. SPECIAL ROOMS AND WARDROBES WERE RESERVED JUST FOR RELAXING AND ENJOYING PIPES.

Most of us don't smoke pipes anymore, and even fewer could devote a whole room to the endeavor. Remember relaxing? Our poor, tired feet should still indulge in the finer things. Sure, we might be drinking tea instead of brandy. Our lounging robes might be cotton, rather than silk. But these are the slippers our butler would fetch for us, if we had one.

Yarn

 Medium

Shown: Touch Me by Muench Yarns, 72% rayon microfiber/28% wool, 1.75 oz (50 g)/ 61 yd (58 m): Red #3620 (MC), 2 (2, 3) balls

Lamé by GGH, 62% rayon cupro/38% polyester, 0.88 oz (25 g)/210 yd (192 m): Gold #100 (CC), 1 ball

Needles

Size 3 (3.25 mm) set of dpn or size to obtain gauge

Notions

Stitch markers

Removable marker

Stitch holders

Tapestry needle

Hand sewing needle and thread

Cardboard for wrapping tassel

Leather or suede scraps for soles (shown: Tandy Leather Factory #5046-04)

Gauge

20 sts and 24 rows = 4" (10 cm) in St st with MC

Take time to check gauge.

Sizes (refer to size chart, page 125)

Woman's S (Woman's M, Woman's L/ Man's S)

Finished size: 8 (8½, 8¾)" (20.5 [21.5, 22] cm) foot circumference, 9 (9½, 10½)" (23 [24, 26.5] cm) foot length

SLIPPER

Instep tab (make 2)

With MC, CO 22 sts.

Rows 1 and 3 (WS): Purl.

Row 2: K5, [k2tog] 6 times, k5—16 sts.

Row 4: [K2tog] 8 times—8 sts.

Row 5 (WS): P8, pick up and purl 3 sts along selvedge edge—11 sts.

Row 6: K11, pick up and knit 3 sts along selvedge edge—14 sts. Break yarn and place sts on holder.

Heel (make 2)

With MC, CO 3 sts.

Next row (WS): P1, p1 and mark this st, p1.

Inc row (RS): Knit to marked st, M1R, k1 (marked st), M1L, knit to end of row—2 sts inc'd.

Rep inc row every RS row 3 more times—11 sts. Work even in St st for 7 rows, ending with a WS row.

Dec row (RS): Knit to 1 st before marked st, s2kp2, knit to end of row—2 sts dec'd.

Rep dec row every RS row 4 more times—1 st. Break yarn and pull through last st.

Foot

With MC and RS of heel facing, beg where last heel st was secured, pick up and knit 26 (28, 30) sts around edge of heel. Work back and forth in St st until piece measures 4½ (5, 5½)" (11.5 [12.5, 14] cm) from pick-up row, ending with a RS row.

Instep

Next row (RS): With RS facing, k14 held sts of instep tab, k26 (28, 30) foot sts, join for working in rnds—40 (42, 44) sts.

Next rnd: K17 (17, 18), pm, k20 (21, 22), pm for new beg of rnd.

Work even in St st until piece measures 6½ (7, 7½)" (16.5 [18, 19] cm) from heel pick-up row.

Toe

Dec rnd: *K1, ssk, knit to 3 sts before marker, k2tog, k1; rep from * once more—4 sts dec'd.

Rep dec rnd every other rnd 4 (4, 5) more times—20 (22, 20) sts. Graft toe, referring to Techniques chapter, page 118, for instructions.

Instep Edging

With RS facing, beg at corner where instep tab meets foot, pick up and knit 55 (59, 63) sts around foot opening, ending at corner where foot meets instep tab. Work 3 rows in k1, p1 rib. BO in patt. Weave in ends, closing gaps between edges of rib and instep tab.

EMBELLISHMENTS

Frog closure (make 2)

With CC, CO 5 sts. Work knitted cord, referring to Techniques chapter, page 122, for instructions, until piece measures 10" (25.5 cm). Break yarn and thread tail through live sts. Fasten securely and pull tail to inside of cord.

Tassel (make 2)

Wrap CC around 2½" (6.5 cm) piece of cardboard 40 times. With hand sewing needle and thread, tie top of tassel firmly, knot, and pull thread ends into tassel. Cut CC ends and remove tassel from cardboard. With CC threaded on a tapestry needle, wrap tassel ½" (1.3 cm) from top. Knot firmly and pull ends under wraps and into tassel. Trim ends evenly.

FINISHING

Form knitted cord into frog as shown, being careful not to twist. Pin in place on slipper toe, tucking ends under. Sew in place with hand sewing needle and thread. Sew tassel in place as shown, both at top and at wrap. Attach leather soles, referring to Techniques chapter, page 116, for instructions.

NIGHT ·········· OWLS

WANNA STAY UP LATE TONIGHT? THEN THESE ARE THE OWLS FOR YOU. MEET "HOOT" AND "HOLLER," THE ORIGINAL NIGHTTIME PARTY ANIMALS.

They know all the best nightspots for big adventures and late-night snacks. Yes siree, from drafty old barns to spooky dark forests, these two can find all the action. And as long as you like eating field mice, you'll love the treats that Hoot and Holler help you find. What's that you say? You'd rather go to bed after all? Well, that's okay. Hoot and Holler will enjoy your share of the mice.

Yarn

 Medium

Shown: Fishermen's Wool by Lion Brand, 100% wool, 8 oz (227 g) /465 yd (425 m): Nature's Brown #150-126, 1 skein

Needles

Size 10 (6 mm) set of dpn or size to obtain gauge

Notions

Stitch markers

Stitch holders

Tapestry needle

Waste yarn for provisional CO

Hand sewing needle and thread

Four 7/16" (11 mm) buttons (shown: La Mode #29895)

Orange and white wool felt scraps

Gauge

16 sts and 22 rnds = 4" (10 cm) in St st, before felting

Take time to check gauge.

Sizes (refer to size chart, page 125)

Child's S (M, L, XL)

Finished size: 6 (6½, 7, 7½)" (15 [16.5, 18, 19] cm) foot circumference, 6 (7½, 8, 8½)" (15 [19, 20.5, 21.5] cm) foot length

Note: Finished size is easily adjusted through blocking.

Construction: Slippers are worked from toe to heel, then felted.

Stitch Guide: S2kp2: Sl 2 sts as if to k2tog, k1, p2sso—2 sts dec'd.

SLIPPER

Toe

Using Judy's magic CO or other toe-up method, CO 20 (20, 24, 24) sts—10 (10, 12, 12) sts on each of 2 dpn. Pm and join for working in rnds.

Next rnd: K10 (10, 12, 12), pm, k10 (10, 12, 12).

Inc rnd: *K1, M1R, knit to 1 st before marker, M1L, k1; rep from * once more—4 sts inc'd.

Rep inc rnd every other rnd 2 (3, 3, 4) more times—32 (36, 40, 44) sts. Work even in St st until piece measures 6½ (8, 8½, 9)" (16.5 [20.5, 21.5, 23] cm) from CO.

Instep

Next rnd: K1 (2, 3, 4), place next 14 sts on holder, turn—18 (22, 26, 30) sts.

Work back and forth in rows. Purl 1 WS row.

Dec row (RS): K1, ssk, knit to last 3 sts, k2tog, k1—2 sts dec'd.

Rep dec row every RS row 1 (2, 3, 4) more time(s)—14 (16, 18, 20) sts.

Sole

Work even in St st until piece measures 10 (13, 14, 15)" (25.5 [33, 35.5, 38] cm) from CO, ending with a WS row. Rep dec row every RS row 2 (3, 4, 5) times—10 sts. Place sts on holder.

EMBELLISHMENTS

Horns

Place 7 held instep sts onto needle. With WS facing, rejoin yarn. Purl 1 WS row.

Dec row (RS): K1, ssk, knit to last 3 sts, k2tog, k1—5 sts.

Purl 1 WS row.

Dec row (RS): K1, s2kp2, k1—3 sts.

Purl 1 WS row.

Dec row (RS): S2kp2—1 st.

Break yarn and pull through last st. Rep for 2nd horn on rem 7 held instep sts.

Edging

With RS facing and beg at center of held sole sts, k5, pick up and knit 22 (28, 30, 33) sts along left edge, *7 sts along side of horn to point, 7 sts along side of horn to base; rep from * once more, 22 (28, 30, 33) sts along right edge, k5 held sts—82 (94, 98, 104) sts. Break yarn and knot to beg of strand.

With waste yarn and using a provisional method, CO 3 sts onto left needle, referring to Techniques chapter, page 120, for instructions. Join working yarn and work 3-st applied cord all the way around slipper, working 3 unattached rows at each horn point, referring to Techniques chapter, page 123, for instructions. Break yarn and graft cord ends tog, referring to Techniques chapter, page 118, for instructions.

FINISHING

Weave in ends. Felt slippers, referring to Techniques chapter, page 114, for instructions. While still damp, shape slippers by hand to proper dimensions, pulling out horn points firmly and cupping heels. Allow to dry completely.

Face

Trace eye and beak templates onto paper and cut out. Trace shapes onto felt pieces in colors as shown and cut out. Pin in place on slipper and sew in place invisibly by hand. Sew on buttons as shown for eyes.

Eye and Beak Templates

OWL EYE

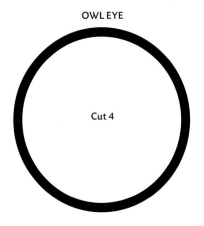

Cut 4

OWL BEAK

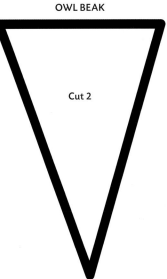

Cut 2

SWORD DANCE ·············

Some mornings, it's harder to face the day than others. For those times when you know a battle is coming, we suggest Sword Dance slippers. Do a few lively steps while the coffee brews, and formulate your plan of attack. The first step to winning a battle is acknowledging that you're in one.

Yarn

 Light

Shown: Socks that Rock Heavyweight by Blue Moon Fiber Arts, 100% superwash merino wool, 7 oz (198 g)/350 yd (320 m): Grawk, 1 skein

Needles

Size 3 (3.25 mm) set of dpn or size to obtain gauge

Size 2 (2.75 mm) 16" (40 cm) circular

Notions

Stitch markers

Removable markers

Stitch holder

Tapestry needle

Size B/1 (2.25 mm) crochet hook

Hand sewing needle and thread

Gauge

24 sts and 36 rows = 4" (10 cm) in St st on larger needles

Take time to check gauge.

Sizes (refer to size chart, page 125)

Woman's S (M, L)

Finished size: 8 (8¾, 9¼)" (20.5 [22, 23.5] cm) foot circumference, 8¾ (9½, 10¼)" (22 [24, 26] cm) foot length

Construction: Slippers are worked from heel to toe.

Stitch Guide: S2kp2: Sl 2 sts as if to k2tog, k1, p2sso—2 sts dec'd.

SLIPPER

Heel (make 2)

With larger needles, CO 3 sts.

Next row (WS): P1, p1 and mark this st, p1.

Inc row (RS): Knit to marked st, M1R, k1 (marked st), M1L, knit to end of row—2 sts inc'd.

Rep inc row every RS row 3 more times—11 sts. Work even in St st until piece measures 1 (1¼, 1½)" (2.5 [3, 4] cm) from CO, ending with a WS row.

Dec row (RS): Knit to 1 st before marked st, s2kp2, knit to end of row— 2 sts dec'd.

Rep dec row every 4th row 2 more times—5 sts. Work 2 rows in St st, ending with a RS row. Place sts on holder.

Foot

With larger needles and RS of heel facing, pick up and knit 33 (37, 41) sts evenly spaced around edge. Work even in St st until piece measures 6 (6½, 7)" (15 [16.5, 18] cm) from pick-up row, ending with a RS row.

Toe

With RS facing, CO 15 sts, join for working in rnds—48 (52, 56) sts.

Next rnd: K5 (6, 7), pm for beg of rnd, k24 (26, 28), pm, knit to end of rnd.

Knit 5 rnds.

Dec rnd: *K2, ssk, knit to 4 sts before marker, k2tog, k2; rep from * once more—4 sts dec'd.

Rep dec rnd every other rnd 5 (6, 7)

more times—24 sts. Arrange sts evenly on 2 dpn. Graft toe, referring to Techniques chapter, page 118, for instructions.

Instep Edging

With smaller needles and RS facing, beg at left of held heel sts, pick up and knit 41 (45, 49) sts along left instep edge, 15 sts along toe CO edge, 41 (45, 49) sts along right instep edge, then k5 held heel sts—102 (110, 118) sts. Pm and join for working in rnds. Work 2 rnds in k1, p1 rib. BO in patt.

EMBELLISHMENTS

Tabs

Fold slipper in half lengthwise. Pm on instep edging at center of toe CO sts and center of heel. Pm in 14th st from each side of center front marker. Pm in every 8th st away from side marker 2 (2, 3) times on each side of slipper— 8 (8, 10) markers. For each tab, with smaller needles and RS facing, pick up and knit 2 sts before marked st, 1 st in marked st, and 2 sts after marked st— 5 sts. Work 12 rows in k1, p1 rib. BO.

Ties (make 2)

With crochet hook, work a crochet chain 5 (5½, 6) feet (1.5 [1.7, 1.8] m) long. Break yarn and pull through last loop.

Tassels (make 4)

Wrap yarn loosely around two fingers 10 times. Tie tassel at top. Wrap 4 times ½" (1.3 cm) from top, securing ends. Cut loops at bottom of tassel. Trim ends evenly.

FINISHING

Weave in ends. Fold each tab to WS, matching end to pick-up row from instep edging. Sew securely in place with hand sewing needle and thread. Thread tie through center front tab of slipper. Match ends evenly and tie in a square knot around center tab. Lace tie through rem side tabs, crossing as shown. Pull tie ends through opposite sides of center back tab as shown. Sew tassels to ends of ties. When worn, ties should cross 3 (3, 4) times on top of foot, then around front, back, and front of ankle before tying.

gOLDFISH

FOR CENTURIES, GOLDFISH HAVE SYMBOLIZED GOOD FORTUNE AND PROSPERITY. THIS ONE IS ESPECIALLY LUCKY:

Make a wish and see if he'll grant it. (Hint: Requests for cozy toes will be fulfilled immediately.) Felted scuffs are the ultimate in fun to make and fun to wear. There's no need to stop after goldfish, either. Embellish the next pair with monograms, flowers, a collection of buttons, or anything else your heart desires. Your wish is our command.

Yarn

 Medium

Shown: Classic Wool Worsted by Patons, 100% wool, 3.5 oz (100 g)/210 yd (192 m): Royal Blue #77132 (MC), 1 skein; Emerald #77708 (CC), 1 skein

Needles

Size 8 (5 mm) 16" (40 cm) circular

Size 10 (6 mm) set of dpn or size to obtain gauge

Notions

Stitch markers

Stitch holder

Tapestry needle

Waste yarn for provisional CO

Hand sewing needle and thread

Orange wool felt scraps

One 4 mm faceted blue bead

Gauge

16 sts and 22 rnds = 4" (10 cm) in St st on larger needles, before felting

Take time to check gauge.

Sizes (refer to size chart, page 125)

Child's S (M, L, XL)

Finished size: 6 (6½, 7, 7½)" (15 [16.5, 18, 19] cm) foot circumference, 6 (7½, 8, 8½)" (15 [19, 20.5, 21.5] cm) foot length

Note: Finished size is easily adjusted through blocking.

Construction: Slippers are worked from toe to heel, then felted.

SLIPPER

Toe

With MC, dpn, and using Judy's magic CO or other toe-up method, CO 24 sts —12 sts on each of 2 dpn. Pm and join for working in rnds.

Next rnd: K12, pm, k12.

Inc rnd: *K1, M1R, knit to 1 st before marker, M1L, k1; rep from * once more—4 sts inc'd.

Rep inc rnd every other rnd 2 (3, 4, 5) more times—36 (40, 44, 48) sts. Work even in St st until piece measures 6 (7½, 8, 8½)" (15 [19, 20.5, 21.5] cm) from CO.

Instep

Next rnd: K5 (6, 6, 7), BO 8 (8, 10, 10) sts, knit to end of rnd, then knit to BO sts, turn—28 (32, 34, 38) sts.

Work back and forth in rows. Purl 1 WS row.

Dec row (RS): K1, ssk, knit to last 3 sts, k2tog, k1—2 sts dec'd.

Rep dec row every RS row 2 (3, 3, 4) more times—22 (24, 26, 28) sts.

Sole

Work even in St st until piece measures 10 (13, 14, 15)" (25.5 [33, 35.5, 38] cm) from CO, ending with a WS row. Rep dec row every RS row 6 (7, 7, 8) times—10 (10, 12, 12) sts. Place sts on holder.

Edging

With smaller needle, CC, RS facing, and beg at center of held sts, k5 (5, 6, 6), pick up and knit 28 (31, 34, 37) sts along left edge, 18 (18, 20, 20) sts along instep edge, 28 (31, 34, 37) sts along right edge, k5 (5, 6, 6) held sts —84 (90, 100, 106) sts. Break yarn and knot to beg of strand. With waste yarn and using a provisional method,

CO 4 sts onto left needle, referring to Techniques chapter, page 120, for instructions. Join CC and work 4-st applied cord all the way around slipper, referring to Techniques chapter, page 123, for instructions. Break yarn and graft cord ends tog, referring to Techniques chapter, page 118, for instructions.

FINISHING

Weave in ends. Felt slippers, referring to Techniques chapter, page 114, for instructions. While still damp, shape slippers by hand to proper dimensions, cupping heels. Allow to dry completely.

Fish

Trace goldfish templates onto paper and cut out. Trace shapes onto felt and cut out. Pin felt pieces in place on slippers so that body aligns when slippers are side by side. Sew in place invisibly by hand. Sew on bead as shown for eye.

Goldfish Templates

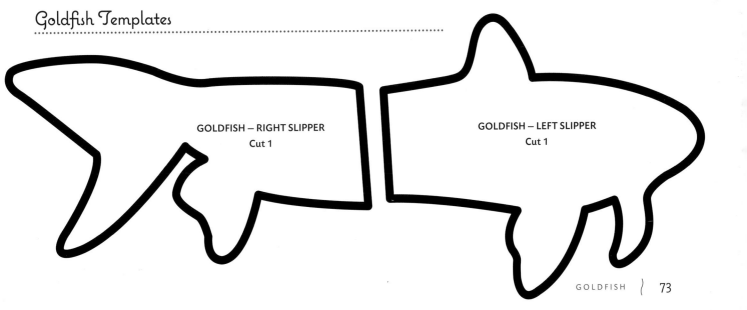

GOLDFISH – RIGHT SLIPPER
Cut 1

GOLDFISH – LEFT SLIPPER
Cut 1

fLOWER GARDEN

SOMETIMES WE NEED A LITTLE INSTANT GRATIFICATION. IN THE DOLDRUMS OF LATE WINTER, WHEN THE FIRST FLATS OF GARDEN PANSIES AND MARIGOLDS APPEAR IN FRONT OF THE GROCERY STORE, I ALWAYS FEEL A LITTLE SURGE OF DELIGHT.

These are flowers I don't have to plant from seeds, or protect through the winter. They appear like magic, with no effort on my part. I can never resist bringing a few home. Flower Garden slippers are just like those first annual blooms. Worked in gigantic plush wool, these darlings will be finished before you can say "begonias." Make some to give away, some to keep for yourself. You can have them right now.

Yarn

 Super Bulky

Shown: Magnum by Cascade Yarns, 100% Peruvian Highland wool, 8.82 oz (250 g)/123 yd (112 m): Lime Heather #9461 (MC), 1 skein; Lake Chelan Heather #9451 (CA), 1 skein; Shire #2445 (CB), 1 skein; Burnt Orange #9465B (CC), 1 skein

Needles

Size 10 (6 mm) set of dpn or size to obtain gauge

Notions

Stitch markers

Removable marker

Tapestry needle

Hand sewing needle and thread

Gauge

12 sts and 20 rows = 4"(10 cm) in St st

Take time to check gauge.

Sizes (refer to size chart, page 125)

Woman's S (M, L)

Finished size: 8 (8¾, 9¼)" (20.5 [22, 23.5] cm) foot circumference, 8½ (9½, 10)" (21.5 [24, 25.5] cm) foot length

Note: Slippers are worked at a firmer gauge than that suggested by the yarn manufacturer.

Construction: Slippers are worked from heel to toe.

Stitch Guide: S2kp2: Sl 2 sts as if to k2tog, k1, p2sso—2 sts dec'd.

SLIPPER
Heel and foot

With MC and using Judy's magic CO or other toe-up method, CO 12 (14, 16) sts—6 (7, 8) sts on each of 2 dpn.

Next row (RS): K6 (7, 8), pm, k6 (7, 8), turn.

Working back and forth in rows, cont as foll:

Row 2 and all WS rows: Sl1p, purl to end of row.

Rows 3, 5, and 7: Sl1k, knit to 1 st before marker, M1R, k2, M1L, knit to end of row—2 sts inc'd and 18 (20, 22) sts after Row 7. Remove marker.

Work even in St st, sl first st of every row, until piece measures 5 (5½, 6)" (12.5 [14, 15] cm) from CO (center back of heel), ending with a WS row. Break yarn.

Instep

With MC and a separate dpn, using the long-tail method, CO 10 sts. Hold instep CO needle with working yarn on the right. Sl last st from foot onto instep CO needle and k2tog with first st of instep CO. Knit to last st of instep CO (8 sts). Sl first st of foot onto instep CO needle and ssk with last st of instep CO, joining rnd, k2 (3, 3), pm, k12 (13, 14), pm for beg of rnd—26 (28, 30) sts.

Next rnd: K1 (1, 2), k2tog, k8, ssk, knit to end—24 (26, 28) sts.

Work even in St st until piece measures 7½ (8, 8½)" (19 [20.5, 21.5] cm) from center back of heel.

Toe

Dec rnd: *K1, ssk, knit to 3 sts before marker, k2tog, k1; rep from * once more—4 sts dec'd.

Rep dec rnd every other rnd 2 (3, 3) more times—12 (10, 12) sts. Graft toe, referring to Techniques chapter, page 118, for instructions.

Instep edging

With RS facing, beg at corner where instep CO sts meet slipper side, pick up and knit 26 (28, 30) sts around instep side edges, ending at corner where slipper side meets instep CO sts. Work 2 rows in k1, p1 rib. BO in patt. Weave in ends, closing gaps between edges of rib and instep CO edge.

GARDEN EMBELLISHMENTS
Large leaf (make 2)

With CB, CO 3 sts.

Next row (WS): P1, p1 and mark this st, p1.

Inc row (RS): Knit to marked st, M1R, k1 (marked st), M1L, knit to end of row—2 sts inc'd.

Rep inc row every RS row once more —7 sts. Work even in St st for 3 rows.

Dec row (RS): Knit to 1 st before marked st, s2kp2, knit to end of row—2 sts dec'd.

Rep dec row every RS row 2 more times —1 st. Break yarn and pull through last st.

Small leaf (make 2)

With CB, CO 3 sts.

Next row (WS): P1, p1 and mark this st, p1.

Work 2 rows in St st. Work 1 dec row as for large leaf—1 st. Break yarn and pull through last st.

Rose (make 2)

With CC, CO 15 sts.

Row 1 (RS): [K1f&b] 15 times—30 sts.

Row 2 (WS): Purl.

BO loosely.

Bobbles (make 6)

With CA, CO 3 sts.

Row 1: Purl.

Row 2: Knit.

BO 2 sts. Break yarn and pull through last st. Also pull CO tail through last st. Pull snugly on working yarn tail to tighten and form bobble.

FINISHING

Weave in ends. Wind rose into a coil as shown. Sew ends in place with hand sewing needle and thread. Block slippers. Sew embellishments in place as shown with hand sewing needle and thread.

rUBY
SLIPPERS ·········

IN THE BOOK *THE WIZARD OF OZ*, DOROTHY'S MAGICAL
SLIPPERS ARE SILVER. FOR THE FILM VERSION, JUDY GARLAND'S
SLIPPERS WERE CHANGED TO RUBY IN ORDER TO SHOW OFF
THE EXPENSIVE NEW TECHNICOLOR TECHNOLOGY.

No one knows how many pairs of ruby slippers were originally
made for the film, but five are known to have survived. One pair
vanished while on loan, never to be seen again. The remaining
four are in private collections and on display at the Smithson-
ian Institute. Their manufacture is attributed to the Western
Costume Company of Hollywood and the original size 5½ shoes
are reported to have cost about $15 a pair in 1938. Their value
today is estimated at $3 million. Dorothy Gale was right, of
course: There's no place like home. Because that's where your
slippers are.

Yarn

 Light

Shown: Alto by Abstract Fiber, 100% blue faced leicester wool, 4.25 oz (120 g)/392 yd (358 m): Solid Red (MC), 1 skein

Sequins 12 by Lucci Yarns, 100% polyester, 0.88 oz (25 g)/100 yd (91 m): Red (CC), 2 skeins

Needles

Size 3 (3.25 mm) set of dpn or size to obtain gauge

Size 2 (2.75 mm) set of dpn

Notions

Stitch markers

Tapestry needle

Hand sewing needle and thread

½ yd (46 cm) of 1¾" (4.5 cm) sequin trim (shown: Simplicity #1862628065)

Gauge

24 sts and 36 rows = 4" (10 cm) in St st with 1 strand of MC and 2 strands of CC held tog on larger needles

Take time to check gauge.

Sizes (refer to size chart, page 125)

Child's S (M, L, XL)

Finished size: 6 (6¾, 7¼, 8)" (15 [17, 18.5, 20.5] cm) foot circumference, 6¾ (7, 7¼, 7½)" (17 [18, 18.5, 19] cm) foot length

Construction: Slippers are worked from heel to toe.

SLIPPER

Heel

With MC, larger needles, and using Judy's magic CO or other toe-up method, CO 20 (24, 24, 24) sts—10 (12, 12, 12) sts on each of 2 dpn.

Next row (RS): K10 (12, 12, 12), pm, k10 (12, 12, 12), turn.

Working back and forth in rows, cont as foll:

Purl 1 row. Join 2 strands of CC and hold with MC.

Inc row (RS): Knit to 1 st before marker, M1R, k2, M1L, knit to end of row—2 sts inc'd.

Rep inc row every RS row 2 (2, 4, 6) more times—26 (30, 34, 38) sts. Remove marker.

Foot

Work even in St st until piece measures 5 (5½, 6, 6½)" (12.5 [14, 15, 16.5] cm) from center back of heel, ending with a WS row.

Toe

With RS facing, CO 10 sts onto right needle—36 (40, 44, 48) sts. Join for working in rnds, k4 (5, 6, 7), pm for beg of rnd, k18 (20, 22, 24), pm, knit to end of rnd. Work even in St st until piece measures ½" (1.3 cm) from instep CO.

Dec rnd: *K1, ssk, knit to 3 sts before marker, k2tog, k1; rep from * once more—4 sts dec'd.

Rep dec rnd every other rnd 5 (6, 7, 8) more times—12 sts. Arrange sts evenly on 2 dpn. Break CC and graft toe with MC only, referring to Techniques chapter, page 118, for instructions.

Instep edging

Turn slipper so that purl side faces out. With smaller needles and MC, pick up and knit 37 (40, 43, 46) sts along left instep edge, 10 sts along instep CO edge, and 37 (40, 43, 46) sts along right instep edge—84 (90, 96, 102) sts. Pm and join for working in rnds. Work 2 rnds in k1, p1 rib. BO in patt.

Tip: Because of the tendency of sequins to stay on the purl side of the work, Ruby Slippers are worked in stockinette stitch with the knit side facing, then turned purl-side out at the end. To keep the slippers smooth and comfortable on the inside, stop every few rows as you work to coax any errant sequins to the purl side.

FINISHING

Weave in ends. Block slippers.

Bow

Cut 2 pieces of sequin trim, each 4½" (11.5 cm) long. Remove loose sequins from cut ends and reserve. Fold each end under ½" (1.3 cm) twice for hem, and sew hem in place with hand sewing needle and thread. Pinch bow to form center pleat and sew in place from WS. Sew bows to slipper toes.

If desired, sew reserved sequins to back of slipper heel to cover CO area.

pENNIES FROM HEAVEN

Moccasin-shaped footwear is an elegant solution to the problem of covering the irregular shape of the human foot. Native American examples beautifully illustrate the basic concept:

A boat-hull-shaped bottom (not unlike a canoe) cradles and covers the bottom of the foot, while an ovoid top piece connects the front sides of the "boat," accommodating the flatter shape of the foot's front. Popular in Norway as early as the 1900s, modern "Aurland Moccasins" were worn all over Europe. The design found its way to America, popularized by *Esquire* magazine and the G. H. Bass company (which added the decorative strip across the instep on their "Weejuns") in the 1930s. By the 1950s, high school and college kids everywhere were wearing moccasins. After some clever soul discovered the instep strap could hold enough change for an emergency phone call, the nickname "penny loafers" stuck. This knitted version is soft and beautiful, made in the traditional shape, with only two main pieces. The decorative instep strap sports cables to frame your pennies. Heavenly!

Yarn

(4) Medium

Shown: Tosh Vintage by Madelinetosh,
100% superwash merino wool, 3.5 oz
(100 g)/200 yd (183 m): Firewood, 2 skeins

Needles

Size 5 (3.75 mm) set of dpn or size to obtain gauge

Size 5 (3.75 mm) 16" (40 cm) circular

Notions

Stitch markers

Stitch holder

Cable needle

Tapestry needle

Hand sewing needle and
thread

Two ½" (13 mm)
flat plastic buttons

Two pennies

Craft adhesive
(such as E6000)

Gauge

24 sts and 32 rows = 4" (10 cm) in St st

Take time to check gauge.

Sizes (refer to size chart, page 125)

Woman's S (Woman's M, Woman's L/
Man's S, Woman's XL/Man's M, Man's L)

Finished size: 9¼ (10, 10¼, 11, 11¼)"
(23.5 [25.5, 26, 28, 28.5] cm) foot
circumference, 8¾ (9½, 10¼, 11, 11¾)"
(22 [24, 26, 28, 30] cm) foot length

Note: Slippers are worked at a
firmer gauge than that suggested
by the yarn manufacturer.

Construction: Slipper soles are
worked from heel to toe; uppers
are worked separately, then
joined to soles.

Stitch Pattern

KEY

☐ k on RS, p on WS

☐ p on RS, k on WS

☑ sl 1 kwise wyib on RS, sl 1 pwise wyif on WS

⬚ 3/3 RC: sl 3 sts onto cable needle,
hold in back, k3, k3 from cable needle

⬚ 3/3 LC: sl 3 sts onto cable needle, hold
in front, k3, k3 from cable needle

CABLE

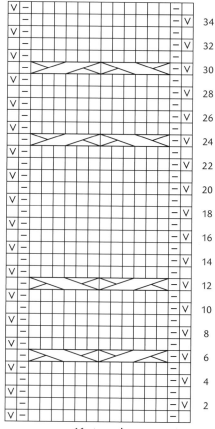

16-st panel

SLIPPER

Heel

Using Judy's magic CO or other toe-up method, CO 24 sts—12 sts on each of 2 dpn.

Next row (RS): K12, pm, k12, turn.

Working back and forth in rows, cont as foll:

Purl 1 row.

Inc row (RS): Knit to 1 st before marker, M1R, k2, M1L, knit to end of row—2 sts inc'd.

Rep inc row every RS row 4 (5, 6, 7, 8) more times—34 (36, 38, 40, 42) sts.

Foot

Work even in St st until piece measures 6½ (7, 7½, 8, 8½)" (16.5 [18, 19, 20.5, 21.5] cm) from CO, ending with a WS row.

Toe

Dec row (RS): Knit to 2 sts before marker, k2tog, ssk, knit to end of row—2 sts dec'd.

Rep dec row every RS row 8 (9, 10, 11, 12) more times—16 sts. Purl 1 row. Arrange sts evenly on 2 dpn. Graft toe, referring to Techniques chapter, page 118, for instructions.

Upper

CO 28 (32, 32, 36, 36) sts. Work 4 rows in k1, p1 rib, ending with a WS row. With WS facing, pick up and purl 4 sts along selvedge edge of piece, turn.

Next row (RS): K4, [k2tog] 14 (16, 16, 18, 18) times, pick up and knit 4 sts along selvedge edge of piece, turn—22 (24, 24, 26, 26) sts.

Work even in St st until piece measures 2¼" (5.5 cm) from CO, ending with a WS row.

Dec row (RS): K2, ssk, knit to last 4 sts, k2tog, k2—2 sts dec'd.

Rep dec row every 4th row 3 (4, 4, 5, 5) more times—14 sts. Place sts on holder.

Instep strap

CO 16 sts. Beg with a WS row, work Rows 1–35 of Cable chart. BO.

FINISHING

Join upper to sole

With circular needle and RS facing, beg at center of heel on sole, pick up and knit 62 (64, 66, 68, 70) sts evenly spaced to center of toe, pm for center front, then 62 (64, 66, 68, 70) sts evenly spaced to center of heel—124 (128, 132, 136, 140) sts. Break yarn. Sl 33 (33, 35, 35, 37) sts from left needle to right needle. Set aside. With dpn and RS facing, beg at lower right edge of upper (but not through ribbed area), pick up and knit 22 (24, 24, 26, 26) sts along side of upper, k7 held sts, pm for center front, k7 held sts, pick up and knit 22 (24, 24, 26, 26) sts along side of upper, ending at rib—58 (62, 62, 66, 66) sts. Do not break yarn. Place upper on top of sole, WS tog, matching center front markers. Beg at left end of upper, join upper to sole using 3-needle BO, referring to Techniques chapter, page 122, for instructions. Work rem 66 (66, 70, 70, 74) sts of sole in k1, p1 rib for 4 rows. BO. Weave in ends, closing gaps between ribbed edge of upper and ribbed edging.

Instep strap

Pin instep strap to upper, aligning edges even with upper seam. Sew edges in place with hand sewing needle and thread. Steam slippers lightly to block. Sew button to center of instep strap through both layers. Attach penny to button with craft adhesive and allow to dry completely before wearing.

Surely You Jest

In stories featuring court jesters, the fool is often the only character with any sense.

It's the clown, the buffoon, who offers sound advice to kings and nobles. Which makes perfect sense: It takes a keen perspective to make a good joke. These are the slippers for when you feel a little foolish. Your wits are at least as sharp as your knitting needles, and the only real fool is the person who takes things too seriously.

Yarn

 Medium

Shown: Classic Wool Worsted by Patons, 100% wool, 3.5 oz (100 g)/210 yd (192 m): Cherry #77710 (CA), 1 skein; Yellow #77615 (CB), 1 skein; Royal Blue #77132 (CC), 1 skein; Emerald #77708 (CD), 1 skein

Needles

Size 4 (3.5 mm) set of dpn

Size 13 (9 mm) 16" (40 cm) circular or size to obtain gauge

Size 13 (9 mm) set of dpn

Notions

Stitch markers

Removable markers

Tapestry needle

Waste yarn for provisional CO

Hand sewing needle and thread

Rubber bands

Gauge

12 sts and 16 rows = 4" (10 cm) in St st with yarn held double on larger needle, before felting

Take time to check gauge.

Sizes (refer to size chart, page 125)

Woman's S (Woman's M, Woman's L/ Man's S, Man's M, Man's L)

Finished size: 10" (25.5 cm) foot circumference, 9 (9½, 10, 10½, 11)" (23 [24, 25.5, 26.5, 28] cm) foot length

Note: Finished foot circumference is easily adjusted through blocking.

Construction: Slippers are worked from heel to toe, then felted.

Stitch Guide: S2kp2: Sl 2 sts as if to k2tog, k1, p2sso—2 sts dec'd.

SLIPPER

Heel (make 2: 1 with CA, 1 with CB)

With 2 strands of yarn held tog and larger needle, CO 3 sts.

Next row (WS): P1, p1 and mark this st, p1.

Inc row (RS): Knit to marked st, M1R, k1 (marked st), M1L, knit to end of row—2 sts inc'd.

Rep inc row every RS row 3 more times—11 sts. Work even in St st until piece measures 7 (7½, 8, 8½, 9)" (18 [19, 20.5, 21.5, 23] cm) from CO, ending with a WS row.

Dec row (RS): Knit to 1 st before marked st, s2kp2, knit to end of row—2 sts dec'd.

Rep dec row every 4th row 4 more times—1 st. Break yarn and pull through last st.

Sides of foot (make 2)

Side 1

With larger needle, waste yarn, and using a provisional method, CO 15 (17, 19, 21, 23) sts, referring to Techniques chapter, page 120, for instructions. With 2 strands of CC held tog, work even in St st until piece measures 7 (7½, 8, 8½, 9)" (18 [19, 20.5, 21.5, 23] cm) from CO, ending with a RS row.

Next row (WS): P7 (8, 9, 10, 11), p1 and mark this st, p7 (8, 9, 10, 11).

Dec row (RS): Knit to 1 st before marked st, s2kp2, knit to end of row—2 sts dec'd.

Rep dec row every RS row 6 (7, 8, 9, 10) more times—1 st. Break yarn and pull through last st.

Side 2

Remove waste yarn from provisional CO and place 15 (17, 19, 21, 23) live sts onto needle. With 2 strands of CD held tog, work as for side 1.

With 2 strands of heel color and tapestry needle, sew sides to heel. Match color change to center bottom of heel and sew 7 (7½, 8, 8½, 9)" (18 [19, 20.5, 21.5, 23] cm) seam.

(continued)

Foot (make 2: 1 with CA, 1 with CB)
Tongue

With larger needle, waste yarn, and using a provisional method, CO 11 sts. With 2 strands of yarn held tog, work in St st until piece measures 2½ (3, 3½, 4, 4½)" (6.5 [7.5, 9, 10, 11.5] cm) from CO, ending with a RS row.

Next row (WS): P5, p1 and mark this st, p5.

Dec row (RS): Knit to 1 st before marked st, s2kp2, knit to end of row —2 sts dec'd.

Rep dec row every 4th row 4 more times—1 st. Break yarn and pull through last st.

Toe

Note: Attach CA toe to foot with CB heel, and attach CB toe to foot with CA heel.

Place markers at edge of foot sides 6½" (16.5 cm) from color change at center bottom of foot. Remove waste yarn from provisional CO and place 11 live sts onto circular needle. With RS facing, rejoin working yarn to tongue, k11 tongue sts, with RS of foot sides facing, pick up and knit 34 sts bet markers—45 sts. Pm and join for working in rnds. Work even in St st until piece measures 2" (5 cm) from pick-up rnd.

Next rnd: *K9, pm; rep from * to end of rnd.

Dec rnd: *K2tog, knit to marker; rep from * to end of rnd—5 sts dec'd.

Rep dec rnd every 4th rnd 6 more times—10 sts. Knit 8 rnds.

Next rnd: [K2tog] 5 times—5 sts.

Knit 8 rnds. Break yarn and thread through rem 5 sts. Pull snugly and thread tail to inside of toe.

EMBELLISHMENTS

Bobbles (make 12: 2 each with CA and CB, 4 each with CC and CD)

With a single strand of yarn, smaller needles, and leaving a 2 yd (2 m) tail, CO 10 sts. Work 10 rows in St st. Break yarn, leaving a 12" (30.5 cm) tail. With tail threaded on a tapestry needle, weave needle around lower 3 sides of square, then through 10 live sts, pulling slightly to gather. Wind CO tail into a ball and place in center of square to stuff. Pull gathering sts firmly to close bobble. Fasten securely, pulling tail to inside of bobble.

Ties (make 4: 2 each in CA and CB)

With a single strand of yarn and smaller dpn, CO 6 sts. Work knitted cord, referring to Techniques chapter, page 122, for instructions, until piece measures 10" (25.5 cm). Break yarn and thread tail through live sts. Fasten securely and pull tail to inside of cord.

FINISHING

Weave in ends. Felt slippers, referring to Techniques chapter, page 114, for instructions. While still damp, curl toe tightly up and over, securing with rubber bands. Stuff slippers with plastic bags, paper, or shoe stretchers, stretching and molding as needed to achieve desired foot length and circumference. Allow to dry.

With hand sewing needle and matching thread, sew CA, CB, CC, and CD bobbles to slipper points as shown. Sew CC and CD bobbles to one end of each tie. Sew other ends of ties to edge of slipper sides as shown. Tie to adjust fit.

αPRÈS SKI

CAN'T MAKE IT TO CHAMONIX THIS YEAR? NOT TO WORRY; YOUR FEET CAN STILL BE AS TOASTY AS AN ALPINE CHALET.

With velvet trim and sparkling beads, these cuddly faux-fur mukluks are fit for the finest fireside. Attach the optional soles and you can even dash outside for more logs. Snuggle up with a hot beverage, and listen to the sound of the falling snow.

Yarn

(**4**) Medium and (**5**) Bulky

Shown: Classic Wool Worsted by Patons, 100% wool, 3.5 oz (100 g)/210 yd (192 m): Black #00226 (MC), 4 skeins

Fun Fur by Lion Brand, 100% polyester, 1.5 oz (40 g)/57 yd (52 m): Lava #320-204 (CC), 4 skeins

Needles

Size 10 (6 mm) 16" (40 cm) circular or size to obtain gauge

Size 10 (6 mm) set of dpn

Notions

Stitch markers

Tapestry needle

Hand sewing needle and thread

2 yd (2 m) of ³⁄₈" (9 mm) burgundy velvet ribbon (shown: May Arts #PV-25)

5 yd (5 m) of ³⁄₁₆" (5 mm) black leather cord (shown: Michaels Crafts Bead Landing Black #146877)

Four 12 mm drum beads (shown: Michaels Crafts Bead Gallery #95798)

Eight 9 mm × 14 mm ruby glass rondelle beads (shown: Michaels Crafts Bead Gallery #93783)

Twenty-six 12 mm lentil beads (shown: Michaels Crafts Bead Gallery #97894)

Eighty 5 mm diamond beads (shown: Michaels Crafts Bead Gallery #97028)

Optional: soles from purchased slippers (shown: Dearfoams #LS067)

Optional: heavy-duty waxed cotton thread

Optional: leather needle

Note: Finished size is easily adjusted through blocking.

Construction: Slippers are worked from toe to top, then felted.

Gauge

16 sts and 22 rnds = 4" (10 cm) in St st with MC, before felting

Take time to check gauge.

Sizes

(refer to size chart, page 125)

Woman's S (M, L, XL)

Finished size: 8 (8½, 9, 9½)" (20.5 [21.5, 23, 24] cm) foot circumference, 9 (9½, 10, 10½)" (23 [24, 25.5, 26.5] cm) foot length

SLIPPER

Toe

With MC and using Judy's magic CO or other toe-up method, CO 24 sts —12 sts on each of 2 dpn. Pm and join for working in rnds.

Next rnd: K12, pm, k12.

Inc rnd: *K1, M1R, knit to 1 st before marker, M1L, k1; rep from * once more—4 sts inc'd.

Rep inc rnd every other rnd 5 (6, 7, 8) more times—48 (52, 56, 60) sts. Remove marker.

Work even in St st until piece measures 9 (9½, 10, 10½)" (23 [24, 25.5, 26.5] cm) from CO.

Gusset

Inc rnd: K24 (26, 28, 30), M1L, knit to end of rnd, M1R—2 sts inc'd.

Rep inc rnd every other rnd 11 (12, 13, 14) more times—72 (78, 84, 90) sts.

Next rnd: K36 (39, 42, 45), pm, knit to last 12 (13, 14, 15) sts, pm, k12 (13, 14, 15)—24 (26, 28, 30) sts between markers.

Heel

Next short-row (RS): Knit to 2nd marker, wrap & turn.

Next short-row (WS): Purl to marker, wrap & turn.

Next short-row: Knit to 1 st before wrapped st, wrap & turn.

Next short-row: Purl to 1 st before wrapped st, wrap & turn.

Rep last 2 short-rows 7 (8, 9, 10) more times—9 (10, 11, 12) wrapped sts at each end, 8 unwrapped sts at center.

Next short-row (RS): Knit to marker, working wraps tog with wrapped sts, turn.

Next short-row (WS): Purl to marker, working wraps tog with wrapped sts, turn.

Next short-row: Sl 1, knit to 1 st before marker, pm, ssk (removing marker), turn—1 st dec'd.

Next short-row: Sl 1, purl to 1 st before marker, pm, p2tog (removing marker), turn—1 st dec'd.

(continued)

Next short-row: Sl 1, knit to marker, ssk, turn—1 st dec'd.

Next short-row: Sl 1, purl to marker, p2tog, turn—1 st dec'd.

Rep last 2 short-rows 10 (11, 12, 13) more times—48 (52, 56, 60) sts. Remove markers.

Leg

Next rnd: K6 (6, 7, 7), pm, *k12 (13, 14, 15), pm; rep from * 2 more times, knit to end of rnd.

Inc rnd: *Work to marker, M1L; rep from * 3 more times, work to end of rnd—4 sts inc'd.

After first inc rnd, hold 1 strand of CC tog with MC and purl every st. Rep inc rnd every 8th rnd 5 more times—72 (76, 80, 84) sts.

Work even in rev St st until piece measures 8 (8½, 9, 9½)" (20.5 [21.5, 23, 24] cm) from beg of CC. Break CC.

With MC, work even in St st until piece measures 4" (10 cm) from last CC rnd. Work 4 rnds in k1, p1 rib. BO loosely.

Tip: Use a hair brush with ball-tipped bristles to gently work as many of the fur fibers as possible to the outside of the boots before felting.

FINISHING

Weave in ends. Felt slippers, referring to Techniques chapter, page 114, for instructions. While still damp, stuff slippers firmly with plastic bags, paper, or shoe stretchers, stretching and molding as needed to achieve desired foot length and circumference. Allow to dry fully before finishing. Attach optional soles if desired, referring to Techniques chapter, page 117, for instructions.

Trim

Beg at center back of mukluk, pin velvet ribbon in place along top edge of fur. Sew in place invisibly by hand. Sew beads in place as shown.

Laces

With MC and a tapestry needle, make guide loops at center back of heel below fur and center front of leg above fur, referring to Techniques chapter, page 120, for instructions. Thread leather cord through lower back guide loop, cross in front and back of boot, then cross ends in front while threading through upper front guide loop. Adjust laces to fit and tie as shown.

Tie a knot about 3½" (9 cm) from each end of cord, thread beads onto cord as shown, then tie a second knot to secure beads. Trim ends if needed.

hEDGEHOGS

How many hedgehogs does it take to make a prickle? At least two, that's for sure. Start your collection with this not-too-prickly pair.

Yarn

![4] Medium and ![5] Bulky

Shown: Fishermen's Wool by Lion Brand, 100% wool, 8 oz (227 g)/465 yd (425 m): Nature's Brown #150-126 (MC), 1 skein

Fun Fur Exotics by Lion Brand, 100% polyester, 1.75 oz (50 g)/55 yd (50 m): Tiger's Eye #320-125 (CA), 1 skein

Fun Fur by Lion Brand, 100% polyester, 1.75 oz (50 g)/64 yd (58 m): Champagne #320-124 (CB), 1 skein

Needles

Size 6 (4 mm) set of dpn or size to obtain gauge

Notions

Stitch markers

Tapestry needle

Four ³⁄₈" (9 mm) buttons (shown: La Petite #735)

Two ⁹⁄₁₆" (13 mm) buttons (shown: La Mode #2065)

Hand sewing needle and thread

Gauge

22 sts and 32 rows = 4" (10 cm) in St st with MC

Take time to check gauge.

Sizes (refer to size chart, page 125)

Child's S (M, L, XL)

Finished size: 6½ (7¼, 8, 8¾)" (16.5 [18.5, 20.5, 22] cm) foot circumference, 6 (7¼, 8, 9)" (15 [18.5, 20.5, 23] cm) foot length

Construction: Slippers are worked from heel to toe.

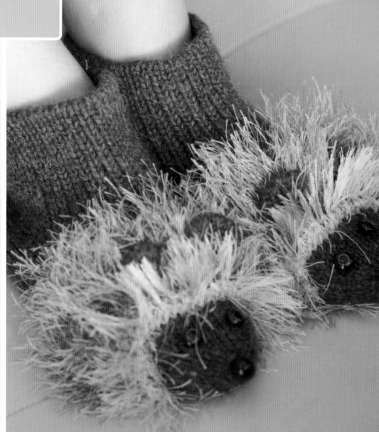

SLIPPER

Heel

With MC and using Judy's magic CO or other toe-up method, CO 12 (16, 20, 24) sts—6 (8, 10, 12) sts on each of 2 dpn.

Next row (RS): K6 (8, 10, 12), pm, k6 (8, 10, 12), turn.

Working back and forth in rows, cont as foll:

Purl 1 row.

Inc row (RS): Knit to 1 st before marker, M1R, k2, M1L, knit to end of row—2 sts inc'd.

Rep inc row every RS row 1 (1, 2, 2) more time(s)—16 (20, 26, 30) sts. Remove marker.

Work in St st until piece measures 2½ (3¼, 3½, 4)" (6.5 [8.5, 9, 10] cm) from center back of heel, ending with a WS row.

Instep

Inc row (RS): K1, M1R, knit to last st, M1L, k1—2 sts inc'd.

Rep inc row every RS row 5 more times —28 (32, 38, 42) sts. With RS facing, CO

8 (8, 6, 6) sts onto right needle and join for working in rnds—36 (40, 44, 48) sts.

Next rnd: K5 (6, 8, 9), pm, k18 (20, 22, 24), pm for new beg of rnd.

Knit 1 rnd. Join 1 strand of CA with MC and purl every rnd until CA section measures ¼ (½, ¾, 1)" (0.5 [1.3, 2, 2.5] cm).

Toe

Dec rnd: *P1, p2tog, purl to 3 sts before marker, p2tog, p1; rep from * once more—4 sts dec'd.

Rep dec rnd every other rnd 2 more times—24 (28, 32, 36) sts. Purl 1 rnd.

Break MC and CA; join 2 strands of CB.

Rep dec rnd—20 (24, 28, 32) sts. Break CB; join 1 strand of MC.

Dec rnd: *K1, ssk, knit to 3 sts before marker, k2tog, k1; rep from * once more—4 sts dec'd.

Rep dec rnd every other rnd 2 (3, 4, 5) more times—8 sts. Break yarn and thread tail through rem sts. Fasten securely on WS.

Cuff

With MC, beg at center back of heel, pick up and knit 13 (16, 18, 21) sts along left edge, 32 sts along instep, and 13 (16, 18, 21) sts along right edge—58 (64, 68, 74) sts. Work in k1, p1 rib until cuff measures 3" (7.5 cm). BO in patt.

EARS (make 4)

CO 8 sts. Pm and join for working in rnds.

Next rnd: K4, pm, k4.

Inc rnd: *K1, M1R, knit to 1 st before marker, M1L, k1; rep from * once more—4 sts inc'd.

Rep inc rnd every other rnd once more—16 sts.

Graft sts tog, referring to Techniques chapter, page 118, for instructions.

FINISHING

Sew larger button to end of slipper toe for nose. Sew smaller buttons in place as shown for eyes. Fold each ear in half vertically to form a pleat and sew in place at CO edge. Sew CO edge to slipper as shown. Weave in ends. Block slippers as desired.

pANDA- MONIUM

FEMALE GIANT PANDAS ARE ABLE TO REPRODUCE ONLY ONCE EVERY TWO TO THREE YEARS, GIVING BIRTH TO ONE, OR SOMETIMES TWO, CUBS.

This slow rate of reproduction, combined with deforestation and hunting in their native China, conspired to reduce their population until they were placed on the endangered species list in 1961. It is estimated that fewer than 1,600 pandas remain in the world, outside captivity.

Newborn pandas are roughly the size of a stick of butter—about 1/900th the size of their mother—but can grow to up to 330 pounds (150 kg) as adults. These bears are excellent tree climbers despite their bulk, and have thickened wrist bones, which allow them to grasp bamboo branches almost as efficiently as if they had thumbs. A fully grown panda can eat 20 to 30 pounds (9 to 14 kg) of bamboo shoots each day. Imagine how much this pair could eat together: Panda-monium, indeed

Yarn

 Medium

Shown: Longwood by Cascade Yarns, 100% superwash extrafine merino wool, 3.5 oz (100 g)/191 yd (175 m): Dew #12 (MC), 1 skein; Ebony #3 (CC), 1 skein

Needles

Size 5 (3.75 mm) set of dpn or size to obtain gauge

Notions

Stitch markers

Tapestry needle

Hand sewing needle and thread

1 yd (1 m) of ⅜" (9 mm) double-faced satin ribbon (shown: Ampelco Ribbon #150-10025)

Two ⁹⁄₁₆" (14 mm) buttons for straps (shown: Dill Buttons #1634)

Four ⅜" (9 mm) buttons for eyes (shown: La Mode #29641)

Gauge

24 sts and 32 rows = 4" (10 cm) in St st

Take time to check gauge.

Sizes (refer to size chart, page 125)

Child's S (M, L)

Finished size: 6 (6¾, 7¼)" (15 [17, 18.5] cm) foot circumference, 6 (7½, 8)" (15 [19, 20.5] cm) foot length

Note: Slippers are worked at a firmer gauge than that suggested by the yarn manufacturer.

Construction: Slippers are worked from toe to heel.

SLIPPERS

Toe

With MC and using Judy's magic CO or other toe-up method, CO 12 sts—6 sts on each of 2 dpn. Pm and join for working in rnds.

Next rnd: K6, pm, k6.

Inc rnd: *K1, M1R, knit to 1 st before marker, M1L, k1; rep from * once more—4 sts inc'd.

Rep inc rnd every other rnd 5 (6, 7) more times—36 (40, 44) sts. Work even in St st until piece measures 2½" (6.5 cm) from CO.

Instep

Next rnd: K6, BO 6 (8, 10) sts, knit to end of rnd, then knit to BO sts—30 (32, 34) sts.

Work back and forth in rows in St st to end of slipper.

Next row (WS): Purl.

Dec row (RS): K1, ssk, knit to last 3 sts, k2tog, k1—2 sts dec'd.

Rep dec row every RS row 3 more times—22 (24, 26) sts. Purl 1 WS row. Change to CC.

Work even until piece measures 4½ (6, 6½)" (11.5 [15, 16.5] cm) from CO, ending with a WS row.

Heel

Next short-row (RS): Knit to last 2 sts, wrap & turn.

Next short-row (WS): Purl to last 2 sts, wrap & turn.

Next short-row: Knit to last 3 sts, wrap & turn.

Next short-row: Purl to last 3 sts, wrap & turn.

Next short-row: Knit to last 4 sts, wrap & turn.

Next short-row: Purl to last 4 sts, wrap & turn.

Next short-row: Knit to last 5 sts, wrap & turn.

Next short-row: Purl to last 5 sts, wrap & turn.

Next short-row: Knit to last 6 sts, wrap & turn.

Next short-row: Purl to last 6 sts, wrap & turn.

Next short-row: Knit to last 7 sts, wrap & turn.

Next short-row: Purl to last 7 sts, wrap & turn.

Next short-row: Knit to last 3 sts, working wraps tog with wrapped sts, ssk, turn.

Next short-row: Purl to last 3 sts, working wraps tog with wrapped sts, p2tog, turn.

(continued)

Next row: Knit to last 2 sts, ssk.

Next row: Purl to last 2 sts, p2tog—18 (20, 22) sts.

Work even in St st until piece measures 4 (5½, 6)" (10 [14, 15] cm) from color change, measured along center of heel, ending with a WS row. Break yarn, leaving sts on needle.

Strap

With CC and a separate needle, CO 15 sts. Work in k1, p1 rib across 15 sts and 18 (20, 22) heel sts, then CO 15 sts—48 (50, 52) sts. Work 2 rows in rib.

First slipper only

Next row (WS): Work in patt to last 5 sts, BO 2 sts for buttonhole, work in patt to end.

Next row: Work 3 sts in patt, CO 2 sts for buttonhole, work in patt to end.

Second slipper only

Next row (WS): Work 3 sts in patt, BO 2 sts for buttonhole, work in patt to end.

Next row: Work in patt to BO sts, CO 2 sts for buttonhole, work in patt to end.

Both slippers

Work 1 row in patt. BO.

Instep edging

With CC and RS facing, beg where strap meets heel, pick up and knit 16 (24, 28) sts along edge of heel (do not break yarn), with MC, pick up and knit 28 (30, 32) sts along MC edge of instep (do not break yarn), with a second strand of CC, pick up and knit 16 (24, 28) sts along edge of heel, ending where heel meets strap—60 (78, 88) sts. Work 3 rows in k1, p1 rib, twisting strands at color changes. BO in patt.

PANDA

Muzzle (make 2)

With MC and leaving an 18" (45.5 cm) tail, CO 21 sts. Pm and join for working in rnds. Purl 1 rnd. Knit 3 rnds.

Next rnd: *K1, k2tog; rep from * to end of rnd—14 sts.

Knit 1 rnd.

Next rnd: *K2tog; rep from * to end of rnd—7 sts.

Break yarn and thread through rem sts. Pull snugly and fasten on WS. Wind CO tail loosely and use to stuff muzzle.

Eye patches (make 4)

With CC, CO 18 sts. Pm and join for working in rnds. Purl 1 rnd. Knit 2 rnds.

Next rnd: *K1, k2tog; rep from * to end of rnd—12 sts.

Knit 1 rnd. Arrange 6 sts on each of 2 dpn. With RS tog, join sts using 3-needle BO, referring to Techniques chapter, page 122, for instructions.

Ears (make 4)

With CC, CO 12 sts. Pm and join for working in rnds.

Next rnd: K6, pm, k6.

Inc rnd: *K1, M1R, knit to 1 st before marker, M1L, k1; rep from * once more—4 sts inc'd.

Rep inc rnd every other rnd once more—20 sts. Knit 2 rnds.

Dec rnd: *K1, ssk, knit to 3 sts before marker, k2tog, k1; rep from * once more—4 sts dec'd.

Rep dec rnd on next rnd—12 sts. Arrange 6 sts evenly on 2 dpn. Graft sts, referring to Techniques chapter, page 118, for instructions.

FINISHING

Weave in ends. Sew muzzle to slipper toe as shown. With CC, embroider nose and mouth on each muzzle as shown. Pin eye patches in place and sew invisibly with hand sewing needle and thread. Pin ears as shown and sew in place. Sew smaller buttons securely to eye patches, through all layers. Sew larger buttons to straps opposite buttonholes. Tie ribbon into bows and sew at base of ears, as shown.

Killer Rab-Boots

"Bunny slippers remind me of who I am. You can't get a swelled head if you wear bunny slippers. You can't lose your sense of perspective and start acting like a star or a rich lady if you keep on wearing bunny slippers.

Besides, bunny slippers give me confidence because they're so jaunty. They make a statement; they say, 'Nothing the world does to me can ever get me so far down that I can't be silly and frivolous.' If I died and found myself in Hell, I could endure the place if I had bunny slippers."

—Dean Koontz

Yarn

4️⃣ Medium and 2️⃣ Fine

Shown: Worsted by Peace Fleece, 80% merino /ramboullet wool, 20% mohair, 4 oz (113 g)/ 200 yd (183 m): Rabbit Gray (MC), 2 (2, 2, 3, 3, 4) skeins; Georgia Rose (CA), 2 mini skeins

220 Sport by Cascade Yarns, 100% Peruvian Highland wool, 1.75 oz (50 g)/164 yd (150 m): Silver Gray #8401 (CB), 1 skein

Small amounts of white and black in worsted weight

Needles

Size 3 (3.25 mm) set of dpn

Size 10 (6 mm) 16" (40 cm) circular or size to obtain gauge

Size 10 (6 mm) set of dpn

Notions

Stitch markers

Removable marker

Tapestry needle

Hand sewing needle and thread

Six 1" (25 mm) buttons (shown: Dill #602)

Four 7/16" (11 mm) buttons (shown: La Mode #29895)

Gauge

16 sts and 22 rnds = 4" (10 cm) in St st with MC on larger needle, before felting

26 sts and 34 rows = 4" (10 cm) in St st with CB on smaller needle

Take time to check gauge.

Note: Finished size is easily adjusted through blocking.

Construction: Slippers are worked from toe to top, then felted.

Stitch Guide: S2kp2: Sl 2 sts as if to k2tog, k1, p2sso—2 sts dec'd.

SLIPPER

Toe

With MC, larger dpn, and using Judy's magic CO or other toe-up method, CO 16 (16, 16, 20, 20, 20) sts—8 (8, 8, 10, 10, 10) sts on each of 2 dpn. Pm and join for working in rnds.

Next rnd: K8 (8, 8, 10, 10, 10), pm, knit to end.

Inc rnd: *K1, M1R, knit to 1 st before marker, M1L, k1; rep from * once more—4 sts inc'd.

Rep inc rnd every other rnd 7 (7, 7, 7, 8, 8) more times—48 (48, 48, 52, 56, 56) sts. Remove marker. Work in St st until piece measures 8 (8½, 9, 9½, 10, 10½)" (20.5 [21.5, 23, 24, 25.5, 26.5] cm) from CO.

Gusset

Inc rnd: K24 (24, 24, 26, 28, 28), M1L, knit to end of rnd, M1R—2 sts inc'd.

Rep inc rnd every other rnd 11 (11, 11, 12, 13, 13) more times—72 (72, 72, 78, 84, 84) sts.

Next rnd: K36 (36, 36, 39, 42, 42), pm, knit to last 12 (12, 12, 13, 14, 14) sts, pm, k12 (12, 12, 13, 14, 14)—24 (24, 24, 26, 28, 28) sts between markers.

Heel

Next short-row (RS): Knit to 2nd marker, wrap & turn.

Next short-row (WS): Purl to marker, wrap & turn.

Next short-row: Knit to 1 st before wrapped st, wrap & turn.

Next short-row: Purl to 1 st before wrapped st, wrap & turn.

Rep last 2 short-rows 7 (7, 7, 8, 9, 9) more times—9 (9, 9, 10, 11, 11) wrapped sts at each end, 8 unwrapped sts at center.

Next short-row (RS): Knit to marker, working wraps tog with wrapped sts, turn.

Next short-row (WS): Purl to marker, working wraps tog with wrapped sts, turn.

Next short-row: Sl 1, knit to 1 st before marker, pm, ssk (removing marker), turn—1 st dec'd.

Next short-row: Sl 1, purl to 1 st before marker, pm, p2tog (removing marker), turn—1 st dec'd.

Next short-row: Sl 1, knit to marker, ssk, turn—1 st dec'd.

Next short-row: Sl 1, purl to marker, p2tog, turn—1 st dec'd.

Rep last 2 short-rows 10 (10, 10, 11, 12, 12) more times—48 (48, 48, 52, 56, 56) sts.

(continued)

Leg

Right slipper only

With RS facing, CO 5 sts onto left needle for underlap, p1, k1, p1, k1, p1, knit to last 5 sts, p1, k1, p1, k1, p1, turn—53 (53, 53, 57, 61, 61) sts.

Left slipper only

Next row (RS): K24 (24, 24, 26, 28, 28), CO 5 sts onto right needle for underlap, turn—53 (53, 53, 57, 61, 61) sts.

Both slippers

Work back and forth in rows.

Next row (WS): K1, p1, k1, p1, k1, purl to last 5 sts, k1, p1, k1, p1, k1.

Next row (RS): P1, k1, p1, k1, p1, knit to last 5 sts, p1, k1, p1, k1, p1.

Cont in patt for 5 more rows, ending with a WS row.

Inc row (RS): Inc 4 sts evenly spaced.

Rep inc row every 8th row 3 more times—69 (69, 69, 73, 77, 77) sts. Work 7 rows even in patt. Work 4 rows in k1, p1 rib. BO in patt.

BUNNY

Outer ears (make 4)

With larger needles and MC, CO 5 sts. Purl 1 row.

Inc row (RS): K1, M1R, knit to last st, M1L, k1—2 sts inc'd.

Rep inc row every RS row once more—9 sts. Rep inc row every 6th row 2 times—13 sts. Work even in St st for 7 rows, ending with a WS row.

Dec row (RS): K1, ssk, knit to last 3 sts, k2tog, k1—2 sts dec'd.

Rep dec row every 4th row 3 more times—5 sts. Purl 1 WS row.

Next row (RS): K1, s2kp2, k1—3 sts.

Purl 1 row.

Next row (RS): S2kp2—1 st.

Break yarn and pull through last st.

Inner ears (make 4)

With larger needles and CA, CO 3 sts. Purl 1 row.

Inc row (RS): K1, M1R, knit to last st, M1L, k1—2 sts inc'd.

Rep inc row every RS row once more—7 sts. Rep inc row every 6th row 2 times—11 sts. Work even in St st for 7 rows, ending with a WS row.

Dec row (RS): K1, ssk, knit to last 3 sts, k2tog, k1—2 sts dec'd.

Rep dec row every 4th row 2 more times—5 sts. Purl 1 WS row.

Next row (RS): K1, s2kp2, k1—3 sts.

Purl 1 row.

Next row (RS): S2kp2—1 st.

Break yarn and pull through last st.

Face (make 2)

With smaller needles and CB, CO 3 sts.

Next row (WS): P1, p1 and mark this st, p1.

Inc row (RS): Knit to marked st, M1R, k1 (marked st), M1L, knit to end of row—2 sts inc'd.

Rep inc row every RS row 8 (8, 8, 9, 10, 10) more times—21 (21, 21, 23, 25, 25) sts. Work even in St st for 7 rows, ending with a WS row.

Dec row (RS): Knit to 1 st before marked st, s2kp2, knit to end of row—2 sts dec'd.

Rep dec row every RS row 6 (6, 6, 7, 8, 8) more times—7 sts.

Rep inc row every RS row 2 times—11 sts.

Work even in St st for 3 rows, ending with a WS row.

Rep dec row every RS row 5 times—1 st. Break yarn and pull through last st.

FINISHING

Weave in ends. Felt slippers and ear pieces (not faces), referring to Techniques chapter, page 114, for instructions. While still damp, stuff slippers firmly with plastic bags, paper, or shoe stretchers, stretching and molding as needed to achieve desired foot length and circumference. Allow to dry fully before finishing.

Face

Pin face to toe of boot and sew in place around edges invisibly by hand. Sew buttons to face as shown. Embroider nose, whiskers, mouth, and teeth as shown.

Ears

Sew one inner ear to each outer ear invisibly by hand. Fold lower ½" (1.3 cm) of each ear under (toward back) and sew in place to form base of each ear. Pin ears to each side of face at top of foot as shown and sew firmly in place around each base.

Tail

Wrap CB around 2" (5 cm) piece of cardboard to make pom-poms. Tie and trim pom-poms. Sew in place as shown.

Closure

Turn boot inside out and tack underlap by hand to WS of boot. Turn RS out and sew buttons to leg above heel as shown, spacing evenly. Make button loops on opposite edge of boot top, referring to Techniques chapter, page 120, for instructions.

тECHNIQUES

CONSTRUCTION NOTES

The projects in this book follow one of two general constructions. Each pattern states which construction type is used.

Heel to Toe

Some heel to toe slippers have a separate heel piece; the slipper sides are either picked up and knit from this piece or sewn to it. Other heels begin with a two-sided cast on (you may be familiar with these from toe-up sock construction) from which the slipper sides are worked back and forth in rows, with centered increases for the heel shaping. After the sides are knit to the desired length, more stitches are cast on and joined for knitting in rounds to cover the foot. Slippers are then shaped with decreases, and the final stitches are grafted together at the toes.

Toe to Heel

These slippers also begin with a two-sided cast on, but are worked in rounds, with increases to shape the foot. Slippers with this construction often cover the whole foot. Heels are shaped either with short rows or flaps and gussets (such as with boots and socks), and may extend all the way up the ankle.

Gauge

In almost every case, the knitted fabric you make for these slippers will be firmer than that suggested by the yarn manufacturer. For this reason, you'll need to be especially careful when making yarn substitutions. To successfully substitute yarns, check the CYCA symbol number listed at the beginning of each pattern, and make sure the yarn you are considering has the same symbol. This way, you can tell whether you are choosing a comparable weight of yarn, regardless of the gauge(s) I have recommended for the project.

For example, the Flower Garden slippers are made from #6 (super bulky) yarn, which has a manufacturer's stated gauge of 8 stitches and 16 rows in 4" (10 cm). For the project,

though, I chose to work the same yarn at a much smaller gauge (12 stitches and 20 rows in 4" [10 cm]) in order to give the slippers more body. In other words, pay attention to the manufacturer's yarn weight when choosing your yarns, and then use the gauge given in the pattern.

Ears, Snouts, and Eyes

Decorative elements for the pieces shown are worked separately and then sewn on by hand. Unless otherwise specified, the pieces should be attached with regular hand sewing thread, in a color to match. Use a doubled strand of thread and sew the pieces on firmly (coating the thread with beeswax is helpful); external bits on slippers are sometimes more prone to coming loose. When an element requires stuffing, an extra length of the project yarn wound into a ball is usually all you need, and has the advantage of not showing through the knitted fabric.

FELTING

Some of the projects in this collection call for you to knit them in a larger-than-usual size and then felt them. Felted knits are much stiffer and more substantial, giving your slippers a sturdy backbone all their own.

There are many ways to felt your knitting, but they all require the same basic elements: water, heat, and agitation. Some pieces, like swatches and small details, are easier to felt by hand. Others are more manageable using a washing machine, due to their size or the yarn you're using. Every yarn will felt differently, so take your time and check on your progress as often as is practical. Remember: Only untreated (nonsuperwash) yarn will felt. Any other non-wool fibers added to the mix will keep your project from succeeding, so check your labels carefully, and if in doubt, use the exact yarn specified in the pattern.

By Hand

Fill a bucket, sink, or bathtub with enough piping hot water to cover your piece, with room to swish it around aggressively. Add a squirt of dishwashing liquid or laundry detergent to remove any residual spinning oils and dirt from the yarn. Wearing rubber gloves will protect your hands as well as provide a little extra traction, particularly if the gloves have textured ridges on the palms. Add your project to the felting bath and let it sit for 20 or 30 minutes to allow the water to penetrate the fibers; this makes the felting go much more quickly. Then scrub, squish, smash, and generally throttle it in the hot water. The length of time you will need to continue this part varies greatly with each yarn type, so check your progress often by squeezing the water out of the piece and evaluating the fabric. Experiment with household utensils, like potato mashers, rubber plungers, and the like, particularly if your hands get tired. Add more hot water and detergent when the bath starts to cool. You can also give your project a "shock" rinse in cold water between baths to further the process.

By Machine

You may have heard that it is not possible to felt your knitting in a front-loading washing machine. While top-loading machines are generally faster, rest assured that they aren't the only way. Front loaders are gentler, and so may take longer, but they will get the job done. To begin, choose the hottest, shortest cycle on your machine. You may need to repeat the cycle, or choose a longer one, but it's safer to work in stages to avoid overfelting.

Place your project into a mesh laundry bag. This is to protect your machine from choking on loose fibers, should the yarn shed too much, and also to keep any small parts from getting lost. Add a pair of jeans or two, and a few clean tennis balls. Washable athletic shoes are also great for felting, particularly if they have rough soles; just be sure to remove the laces first. Use regular laundry detergent, but don't add liquid fabric softener. Start the machine and let the magic begin. After the machine has filled with water, stop the cycle and let the project sit for 20 or 30 minutes to allow the water to penetrate the fibers; this makes the felting go much more quickly. After resuming the cycle, check your project from time to time, if your washer allows (it's hard to stop a front-loading machine mid-cycle), to evaluate the felting.

Whether you felt by hand or by machine, you'll be able to tell the felting is complete when your piece matches the finished dimensions indicated in the pattern (or a bit smaller—you can always stretch felted items somewhat, but if they're too big, you can only do more felting). Generally speaking, the knitted stitches should no longer be defined, the surface of the fabric should have a fuzzy "halo," and the fabric should be smooth and even when you are done. If any of these properties is absent, but the size is correct, stop felting. If all these characteristics are present but the piece is still too large, felt some more.

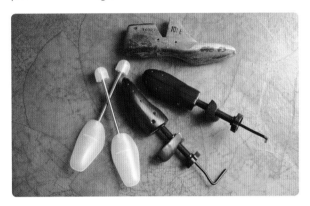

Blocking Felt

Once your pieces are felted, you'll need to stretch, mold, and manipulate them into shape. Shoe trees, shoe stretchers, and wadded paper and plastic bags all make great felted slipper forms. Check your kitchen utensil collection for serving spoons and other tools that can be used to stretch and shape heels and toes. Use rolled washcloths, sewing pins, and even duct tape to get your slipper form to just the right size and shape. Place the damp slippers over their forms, stretching and smoothing them into shape. Pin flat pieces down on an ironing or blocking board. This is the time to apply steam from your iron if you need to manipulate the felt even more. Let the pieces air-dry completely before final finishing. If you aren't happy with the final result after blocking, don't hesitate to wet the piece again and start over. Unlike regular knitting, felted knits can withstand aggressive blocking, and even look better for it.

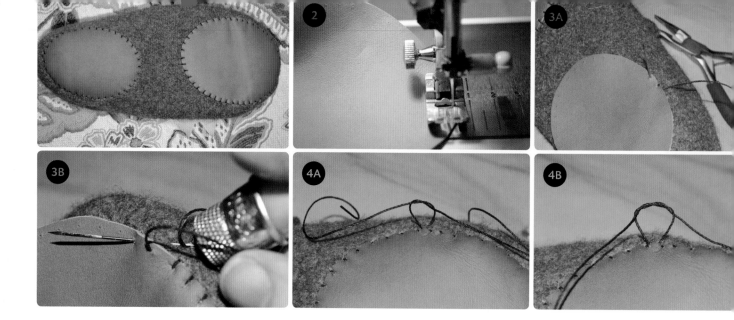

ADDING SOLES

Any of the designs in this book can have soles attached, for greater comfort and durability. There are many ways to sole your slippers, but the three techniques shown in this collection are split leather soles, full leather soles with chipboard, and purchased rubber soles.

Leather Soles (above)
(see also Smoking Slippers, page 58)

1. On a piece of scrap paper, trace around the finished slipper. You can either use this tracing as is for a full sole, or you can make split soles, as shown here. The advantage to split soles is that they require less leather and they leave part of the slipper sole exposed. This is a good thing if you ever have to wash your slippers; they can be more easily dried and reshaped with less leather on the bottoms. To make split soles, draw a large oval over your tracing at the top (toe and ball of foot), and a smaller one at the bottom (heel). Cut out the ovals and trace each one onto the wrong side of some leather scraps, twice.

2. To make the leather easier to manage, poke holes all the way around each piece. A punch or an awl works fine for this. If you have a sewing machine, try this trick: Install a leather needle, without any thread in the top or bobbin of the machine. Set the stitch length to the longest possible setting, and carefully "sew" all around the edge of each sole piece. Voilà! Perfectly spaced stitching holes.

3. Hold the leather piece against the bottom of the slipper. Leave about 6" (15 cm) of thread, without knotting, and start stitching around the oval (A).

   To sew the soles on, use a hand sewing leather needle and heavy waxed cotton thread. The tip of the leather needle is an extremely sharp, triangular lance, so don't pull it with your fingertips. Instead, push it from the eye end with a thimbled finger as far as you can, then pull it the rest of the way through with small pliers. A simple edge stitch (B) works fine, or if your stitching holes end up farther inside the edge of the oval, a blanket stitch will keep the edges of the leather from curling.

4. End with a surgeon's knot. Cross the thread ends as for a square knot (A). Cross the thread ends *twice* and pull tight (B).

Full Leather Soles with Chipboard
(shown on Turkish Delight, page 42)

Adding a full leather sole is just the same as a split one, except that there will be only one piece of leather for each slipper. In the case of some scuff slippers, you'll need to add a stiffener to the soles. Chipboard is an inexpensive, stiff cardboard that can be found at craft stores, and it is easy to cut and shape.

1. On a piece of scrap paper, trace around the finished slipper sole. Cut out the tracing, and copy onto the wrong side of leather. Draw another line outside the tracing line, approximately ¼" (6 mm) away. Cut along the outside line. Make two.

2. Trace around the paper twice again, this time onto the chipboard, and cut out. Layer the chipboard between the slipper sole and the leather and stitch the leather in place as for split soles.

Purchased Rubber Soles (right)
(shown on Après Ski, page 92)

For even greater durability, reuse the soles from inexpensive purchased slippers for your handmade ones. Drugstores and variety stores offer cheap slippers in all sizes, particularly in the fall and winter months. Look carefully to make sure the slippers you are considering have real thread stitching holding the soles to the uppers. Many are held on with only glue and have artificial "stitches" molded into the edge of the sole.

1. When you get them home, use a seam ripper to carefully remove the soles and insoles from the uppers. If your slippers have foam padding between the sole and the insole, save it for reuse; it's already cut to the perfect shape.

2. Layer the soles, insoles, and your slippers together and stitch through the original holes in the soling material. Use heavy waxed cotton thread and a hand leather needle with thimble and pliers, as for with leather soles. Be sure to stitch all the way through the knitting and

then back out again. If necessary, stitch a second time all the way around the sole using the alternate holes, for a smooth, tight fit.

After applying the soles of your choice, consider adding padded insoles from the drugstore to your slippers. The extra layer of padding is luxurious, extends the life of your slippers, and is easy to remove for washing or replacement. Padded insoles even allow them to step outdoors from time to time.

USEFUL STITCHES

Kitchener Stitch/Grafting (below)

Kitchener stitch, also known as grafting, is the seaming method of choice when you need to join a row of live stitches to a second row of live stitches. It produces a seam that's virtually undetectable. To help demonstrate the steps, a contrasting yarn has been used in the photos.

1. Cut the working yarn, leaving a tail about 18" (46 cm) long. Leave the stitches on the needles; there should be the same number of stitches on each. Hold the needles side by side in the left hand, with the right side facing up. Slide the stitches toward the needle tips. Arrange so that the working yarn is coming from the first stitch on the back needle. Thread the yarn tail onto a yarn needle. Draw the yarn through the first stitch on the front needle as if to purl, and leave the stitch on the needle.

2. Keeping the yarn under the needles, draw the yarn through the first stitch on the back needle as if to knit, and leave the stitch on the needle.

3. Draw the yarn through the first stitch on the front needle as if to knit, and slip the stitch off the needle. Draw the yarn through the next stitch on the front needle as if to purl, and leave the stitch on the needle.

4. Draw the yarn through the first stitch on the back needle as if to purl, and slip the stitch off the needle. Draw the yarn through the next stitch on the back needle as if to knit, and leave the stitch on the needle.

5. Repeat steps 3 and 4 until all but the last two stitches have been worked off the needles. Insert the tapestry needle knitwise into the stitch on the front needle, and purlwise into the stitch on the back needle, slipping both stitches off their respective needles. Stretch out your seam or use the tip of a needle to adjust stitches a bit and even out the tension in the yarn.

Duplicate Stitch (above)

Start your duplicate stitching by reading the chart as you would to knit. Start at the right bottom corner of the design.

1. Thread your yarn onto a large-eye tapestry needle.

2. From the wrong side bring your needle to the right side, through the stitch below where the first stitch is to be made.

3. Pass the needle from right to left under the stitch above.

4. Dive the needle into the same hole where you first brought the yarn up.

5. Bring your needle to the right side, into the center of the next stitch to the left. Work as in steps 3 and 4.

6. Continue in this manner for the number of stitches needed.

If your chart moves you to the next row above, you will work left to right. This is often easier if you turn your work upside down. For the next row, turn your work right side up again, and continue in this manner.

You will see as you make your duplicate stitches that you are exactly mimicking your base knitting. For the best results, dive your needle up and down for each step of the duplicate stitch. This way the new color will lie directly on top, giving good coverage of the base stitch.

Buttonhole Stitches and Button Loops

The same sewing technique is used to reinforce the edges of a buttonhole and to create button or guide loops. Only the material being stitched on and the distance between the stitches are different.

Buttonholes
Blanket Stitch (below)

To work blanket stitch over an edge, bring the needle up through the edge to be covered. Make a vertical stitch, bringing the needle through the loop formed by the working strand as shown. Pull snug against the edge. Space subsequent stitches ⅛" to ¼" (3 to 6 mm) apart.

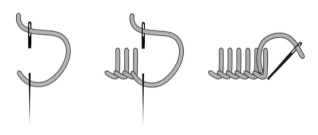

Button/Guide Loops

1. Using a yarn needle threaded with a double strand of yarn, make a straight stitch long enough for the button or trim to pass under. Bring the needle back up at the beginning of this stitch. Pass the needle under the foundation yarn, then through the loop formed by the working strand, and pull tight.

2. Continue making stitches, pushing each tightly up next to the last and pulling firmly until the foundation loop is completely covered. Secure the yarn end and trim.

Short-Rows

When working short-rows, you shape the knitting by working partway through a row, then turning the work and going back the other way. There are many ways to work short-rows, one of which is the "wrap and turn" method.

It involves two stages. The first is wrapping and turning, in which you wrap the working yarn around a stitch at the turning point to avoid leaving a hole in the work. The second stage is completed the next time that stitch is worked, when you pick up the wrap and work it together with a live stitch in order to hide it.

Wrap and Turn

1. Work the row for the specified number of stitches, either knitting or purling.

2. Slip the next stitch purlwise.

3. Bring the yarn between the needles to the other side of the work and slip the same stitch to the left-hand needle.

4. Turn. Purl or knit the next stitch as specified.

Pick Up Wraps

To knit a wrapped stitch, insert the needle from the bottom to the top, front to back, under the wrap, then knitwise into the wrapped stitch. Knit the wrap and the stitch together.

To purl a wrapped stitch, insert the needle from the bottom to the top, back to front, under the wrap, then purlwise into the wrapped stitch. Purl the wrap and the stitch together.

CAST-ON TECHNIQUES
Provisional Cast On (above, opposite)

There are many kinds of provisional cast ons. This one is included because it's easy to remove.

1. Choose a smooth, durable waste yarn (cotton works well) and any medium-size crochet hook.

2. With waste yarn, make a slip knot and place on the crochet hook. Hold the hook in your right hand and a knitting needle in your left.

3. With the crochet hook above the needle and the working yarn below it (A), wrap the yarn around the hook and pull through the slip knot (B). Bring the working yarn to the back, under the needle (C).

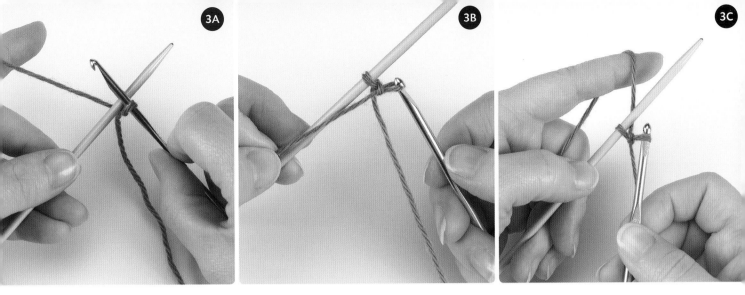

4. Repeat step 3, pulling the yarn through the new loop on the hook, until there is one fewer stitch than required on the needle.

5. Move the loop from the hook to the needle. Break the waste yarn. Knit one row with the working yarn to complete the cast on.

To remove waste yarn, loosen the end of the chain and pull through the end of the last chain stitch. Gently pull on the tail of the waste yarn to release one live knitting stitch at a time, placing on the needle.

Judy's Magic Cast On

Initially conceived for use in toe-up sock knitting, this cast on is useful for pieces that are worked from a closed end to an open one. Use two double-pointed needles to work the cast on (visit http://knitty.com/ISSUEspring06/FEAT-magiccaston.html for detailed instructions and photos).

1. Make a slip knot and place the loop around one needle. This is the first stitch.

2. Hold both needles parallel in your right hand, the needle with the slip knot on top. The upper needle is #2 and the lower needle is #1.

3. In your left hand, hold the yarn so that the tail goes over your index finger and the working end goes over your thumb.

4. Bring the tip of needle #1 over the strand of yarn on your finger, around and under the yarn and back up, making a loop around needle #1, pulling yarn snug— 1 stitch on needle #1.

5. Bring needle #2 over the yarn tail on your thumb, around and under the yarn and back up, making a loop around needle #2, pulling yarn snug—2 stitches on needle #2.

The top strand always wraps around the lower needle (#1), and the bottom strand always wraps around the upper needle (#2).

6. Repeat steps 4 and 5 until the desired number of stitches is cast on, ending with step 4.

7. To work the first round, rotate the needles so that #1 is on top, and begin knitting. When all the stitches from needle #1 have been worked, you will see a row of stitches appear between the two needles. Continue knitting across needle #2, working the stitches through the back loop so that they aren't twisted. Incorporate additional double-pointed needles as the piece grows.

THREE-NEEDLE BIND OFF (above)

This technique joins any two sets of live stitches into a secure and bulk-free seam. It only works when the two pieces contain the exact same number of stitches to be joined.

1. Place one set of live stitches onto each of two needles. Hold the pieces to be joined in your left hand with right sides together.

2. With your right hand, insert a third needle through the first stitch on each needle. Wrap the working yarn, then pull the new stitch through both the old ones, slipping them off their needles.

3. Work the next stitches from each needle together, then pass the first stitch on the right needle over the second to bind off.

4. Repeat step 3 until all stitches from both pieces are worked. Break working yarn and pull tail through last loop.

CROCHETED AND KNITTED CORDS
Crocheted Chain

1. Make a slip knot and place on a crochet hook.

2. Bring the yarn over the hook from back to front and grab it with the hook.

3. Draw the hooked yarn through the slip knot and onto hook—1 chain stitch is complete.

4. Repeat steps 2 and 3, pulling the hooked yarn through the new loop on the hook, until the chain reaches the desired length. Break yarn and pull tail through last stitch.

Knitted Cord (below, opposite)

Sometimes referred to as I-Cord ("Idiot Cord"), knitted cord is made by working a small number of stitches on double-pointed needles without turning the work. The resulting piece is a narrow tube of knitting. Knitted cord can be worked either independently or knitted onto another piece as an edging (see Applied Knitted Cord, page 123).

1. Using two double-pointed needles, cast on the required number of stitches. The knitted cord can be worked in any gauge, and with any number of stitches, depending on the thickness or fineness of the cord required.

2. Knit all the stitches. At the end of the row, rather than turning the work, slide all the knitted stitches to the opposite end of the needle (A), draw the working yarn across the back of the work snugly, then knit all the stitches again (B).

3. Continue sliding and knitting until the cord is the desired length.

4. Break the working yarn and thread through a tapestry needle. Thread the yarn tail through all the live stitches and pull snugly to close. Pull the tail through the inside of the cord to hide it.

Applied Knitted Cord

There are two ways to apply a knitted cord to another piece of knitting. The method you choose will depend on whether the piece to be edged has live stitches available.

Live Stitches

1. With all live stitches still on the needle and right side facing, cast on the specified number of cord stitches at the beginning of the next row.

2. Knit to the last cord stitch.

3. Ssk the last cord stitch together with the next live stitch.

4. Transfer (slip as if to purl) all cord stitches to the left-hand needle.

5. Repeat steps 2 through 4 until all live stitches from the edge have been worked.

6. Break working yarn and thread tail through cord stitches. Pull snugly to close and weave end to inside of cord.

Pick Up and Knit

1. With yarn to match cord, pick up and knit stitches through the edge to which the cord is to be attached. Cast on the specified number of cord stitches at the beginning of the row.

2. Follow steps 2 through 4 for live stitches.

3. When applying knitted cord around an entire edge, graft the ends of the cord together (see Kitchener Stitch/Grafting, page 118).

abbreviations

[ ]	work instructions between brackets as many times as directed
*	repeat instructions following the asterisk as indicated
"	inches
approx	approximately
beg	begin(ning)
BO	bind off
CA	color A
CB	color B
CC	color C or contrasting color
cm	centimeter(s)
CO	cast on
cont	continue
dec	decrease(s)(ing)
dpn	double-pointed needle(s)
foll	following
g	gram
inc	increase(s)(ing)
k	knit
kwise	knitwise
k2tog	knit two stitches together
LH	left hand
m	meter(s)
MC	main color
M1L	make one left
M1R	make one right
oz	ounce(s)

p	purl
patt(s)	pattern(s)
pm	place marker
prev	previous
pwise	purlwise
p2sso	pass two slipped stitches over
p2tog	purl two stitches together
rem	remain(s)(ing)
rep	repeat(s)
rev St st	reverse stockinette stitch
RH	right hand
rnd(s)	round(s)
RS	right side
sl	slip
sl1p	slip one stitch purlwise
ssk	[slip one stitch knitwise] two times, work these two stitches together
ssp	[slip one stitch knitwise] two times, transfer two stitches to left needle, purl two stitches together through back loops
st(s)	stitch(es)
St st	stockinette stitch
tbl	through back loop
tog	together
WS	wrong side
yd(s)	yard(s)
yo	yarn over

resources

Abstract Fiber
3673 SE Martins Street
Portland, OR 97202
www.abstractfiber.com

Blue Moon Fiber Arts
56587 Mollenhour Rd
Scappoose, OR 97056
www.bluemoonfiberarts.com

Cascade Yarns
1224 Andover Park E
Tukwila, WA 98188
cascadeyarns.com

Lion Brand Yarn
135 Kero Road
Carlstadt, NJ 07072
lionbrand.com

Lucci Yarns
202-91 Rocky Hill Road
Bayside, NY 11361
lucciyarn.com

Madeline Tosh
7515 Benbrook Parkway
Benbrook, TX 76126
madelinetosh.com

Muench Yarns/GGH
1323 Scott Street
Petaluma, CA 94954
www.muenchyarns.com

Patons Yarns
320 Livingstone Avenue South
Listowel, ON
Canada N4W 3H3
www.yarnspirations.com/patons

Peace Fleece
475 Porterfield Road
Porter, ME 04068
www.peacefleece.com

SLIPPER SIZE CHARTS

CHILD	Child Small (3–5 years)	Child Medium (5–9 years)	Child Large (7–13 years)	Child X-Large (13 years-adult)
Foot Circumference	6" (15 cm)	6½" (15.5 cm)	7" (18 cm)	7½" (19 cm)
Foot Length (Heel to Toe)	6" (15 cm)	7½" (19 cm)	8" (20 cm)	8½" (22 cm)

ADULT	Woman's S	Woman's M	Woman's L Man's S	Woman's XL Man's M	Man's L	Man's XL
Foot Circumference	8" (20 cm)	8½" (21.5 cm)	9" (23 cm)	9½" (24 cm)	10" (25 cm)	11" (28 cm)
Foot Length (Heel to Toe)	9" (23 cm)	9½" (24 cm)	10" (25 cm)	10½" (26.5 cm)	11" (28 cm)	12" (30.5 cm)

αBOUT THE AUTHOR

MARY SCOTT HUFF lives in Fairview, Oregon, and teaches knitting all over the United States. Mary designs knitwear, writes books, blogs, and generally pursues a yarn-centered existence, in a little red house shared with her husband, two children, and two Scottish Terriers. This is her fourth book. Join Mary in her adventures playing with string at www.maryscotthuff.com.

acknowledgments

My sincere thanks to everyone who leant their talents and support to this project.

The Lindas: both Neubauer and Rhogaar, for continuing to believe in me, even when I asked questions like "Which end of the lobster would you put your foot inside?"

Karen Frisa, whose patience and skill result in patterns that are coherent and knittable, even though they come from inside my head.

Lisa Kobek, who didn't flinch when I brought a giant unfelted slipper to her wedding reception so I could ask her a question.

My readers and students, for their unfailing candor, and unselfish sharing of big ideas.

All of the generous yarn makers, who understand that a world without string is chaos.

Phillip, Lindsay, and Campbell Huff, for not arguing when I told them frozen dinners are a food group and not complaining when Mount Washmore surpassed all previously recorded heights. Likewise, Paisley and Bailey, for their constant supervision and for always making room on the sofa for more yarn.